Media Selection Handbook

Media
Selection
Handbook

Mary Robinson Sive

LIBRARIES UNLIMITED, INC.
Littleton, Colorado
1983

LIBRARIES UNLIMITED, INC.
P. O. Box 263
Littleton, Colorado 80160-0263

Library of Congress Cataloging in Publication Data

Sive, Mary Robinson, 1928-
   Media selection handbook.

   Includes bibliographical references and index.
   1. Audio-visual materials--Catalogs. I. Title.
LB1043.Z9S58   1983   011   83-932
ISBN 0-87287-350-1

Libraries Unlimited books are bound with Type II nonwoven material that meets and
exceeds National Association of State Textbook Administrators' Type II nonwoven
material specifications Class A through E.

211612

Foreword

Much has been written on the design and production of instructional materials, as well as the selection of materials for use with individual learners. Much is also available on the selection process for library collections, covering traditional items of books, periodicals, and films. Few sources, however, have addressed the special problems of selecting and collecting other types of instructional materials, including filmstrips, slides, and much more. Kits, games, and realia are bibliographically elusive. They seldom are reviewed; previewing opportunities are limited; and producer catalogs remain the chief source of information, giving availability, but providing little accurate guidance about quality.

Now Mary Sive, author of three editions of *Selecting Instructional Media*, has turned her experienced attention to the process of developing media collections which fully support educational programs. This text provides a summary of the most useful bibliographic tools for these evasive materials, as well as a series of case studies demonstrating sensible procedures for the identification and verification of appropriate media. As one who teaches courses on the selection and utilization of instructional materials, I find this a new approach and a welcome addition to collection development literature.

Jane C. Terwillegar

Preface

The practicing media specialist, working under the pressure of time, can rarely afford the luxury of lengthy and exhaustive selection. Decisions about what to recommend for purchase must often be hurried, but need not be haphazard.

Knowing the most dependable aids for making choices and how to use them to the best advantage can make the selection process deliberate, goal-oriented, and satisfactory to those concerned—the teachers and students who are the ultimate consumers, the media specialist who seeks to serve them, and the administrator who must be accountable to taxpayers.

Media specialists are information managers, and this volume aims to assist them in that function by identifying the most essential selection tools and describing what each can and cannot do. *Media Selection Handbook* is dedicated to helping building-level and district personnel develop collections that can help teachers implement curriculum objectives and make "best fit" decisions. Its objectives are 1) to reduce the work load of the library/media specialist by omitting selection procedures that lead to programs neither needed nor affordable, 2) to reduce teacher-librarian tensions, and 3) to encourage the use of school media centers.

Media Selection Handbook gives detailed directions for the systematic detection of specific needs and for systematic comparison shopping that identifies available, relevant media and assesses their quality in relation to cost and potential usage. Its scope is limited to nonprint media exclusive of films and to instructional uses at levels from kindergarten through community college.

Three separate parts make up this handbook. Part I briefly summarizes principles of media use, media selection, and instructional development. A chart provides a quick glance at selection criteria promulgated by leading national organizations. Part II takes up certain selection tools in turn, describing the features of each in detail, reproducing sample pages, and offering specific directions for usage. Figures highlight the special utility of each. Optimal paths for current and retrospective searches are suggested in part III, and examples demonstrate specific applications of the procedures suggested in the previous chapters.

The fifteen tools recommended in part II, if regularly consulted, will help with choosing a variety of formats, including:

> filmloops
> filmstrips (sound and silent or captioned)
> kits (defined as two or more media not necessarily used together
>   or coordinated)
> pictorial and graphic materials (study prints, photographs, and
>   similar products requiring no projection equipment)
> simulation games

slides (photographic slides and slide-tape sets)
sound recordings (discs, tapes, cassettes)
transparencies
videorecordings (tapes, cassettes, discs)

Nine of the tools are appropriate for all instructional levels, three for elementary only, and three for secondary and up. It is recommended that the media center director keep titles that are in frequent use at the desk, and identify and establish working relationships with close-by sources for access to others.

Books and 16mm films have been omitted from this text because book selection is thoroughly covered in many other sources, and book reviews and *Books in Print* are widely available. Film reviews and filmographies are also relatively plentiful. Moreover, media or learning resources centers can look to public libraries to supplement book collections, but may in the future be expected to share their unique nonprint resources with the community at large. Individual building media centers rarely purchase films in any case, typically renting them from district, regional, or state film libraries.

"Media" are defined by the Association for Educational Communications and Technology/American Association of School Librarians as "all of the forms and channels used in the transmittal of information process," i.e., including print. For the purposes of this work, the term is more narrowly employed to encompass the particular formats enumerated above. Except for the omission of films, this is close to colloquial usage. "Audiovisual media" and "audiovisual materials" are also employed, with synonymous intent. "Nonprint" as an alternative is unappealing; one hesitates to define anything as what it is *not*. "Media center," "learning center," "resources center," and "instructional materials center" are used interchangeably.

"Selection is a complex decision-making process that involves . . . juggling . . . need, effectiveness and costs," states Woodbury (*Selecting Materials for Instruction*, Libraries Unlimited, 1980, p.22). It is also an ongoing process of interaction between media specialists and classroom personnel. It is a process that starts with needs, not habits or impulse buying, and one that calls upon all the creative problem-solving skills the selector can muster. To solve a problem, it must first be formulated, then a plan of action developed. The pages that follow outline this process.

Selection of audiovisual materials rarely gets more than cursory treatment in texts on media center operation and audiovisual instruction. This volume hopes to supplement their counsel with practical suggestions.

The selection aids discussed here are culled from the more than 500 that are annotated and mentioned in the author's *Selecting Instructional Media*, 3rd edition (those cover films, free and inexpensive publications, and government publications as well). Free-loan media are outside the scope of this book and are mentioned only incidentally. Where needed, readers may extend the titles described here with mediagraphies, both on specific subjects and of specific formats in that work. The introductory "Essay on Media Selection" in *Selecting Instructional Media*, 3rd edition, augments the observations in the following chapters and offers an extensive bibliography of writings on media selection.

Thanks are due to the publishers and other organizations who gave permission to reprint and supplied photographs and other visuals.

This text reflects what the author has learned in some thirteen years of involvement with instructional media—first as a school librarian in the 1960s and later as a writer on the subject. All my professional contacts during that period contributed to my learning. They included first-graders whose names I no longer remember, fellow teachers, principals, superintendents, fellow school board members, professors, editors, and publishers. I would like to single out for special thanks Professor Diana L. Spirt, Palmer Graduate Library School, Long Island University, for friendship and support, and Jane C. Terwillegar for shared ideas and commitments. I alone am responsible for any errors.

Table of Contents

List of Figures

Figures

PART I _____

The principles that govern instructional development and individualized instruction for all students, including the exceptional, provide the foundation for effective media selection. The chapters in part I summarize those principles, following a brief examination of the present status of media selection. A selection process that begins with assessment of needs and seeks to implement cost-effectiveness is then recommended.

Media in Education —
A Promise That Failed?

During the heyday of the "back to basics" movement, the belief was widespread that our schools' infatuation with educational technology was over, replaced by a universal return to the textbook as the core mode of instruction after years of multimedia exposure. The presence of microcomputers in schools everywhere makes it clear that educators continue to look to technology to facilitate the task of instruction and to improve its quality. Even more far-reaching technologies are on the horizon—interactive access via these same microcomputers to mini-libraries in all formats stored on videodiscs; exciting learning programs which can be brought into schools as readily as video games have invaded neighborhood grocery stores.

Audiovisual instruction becomes an easy target of budget-cutting. Administrators see collections that still contain many titles that are leftovers from 1960s federal funding. Contending that media are as yet unproven, they refuse to allocate budget funds to buy more up-to-date materials. (In this Catch-22 situation, fifteen- or twenty-year-old filmstrips will certainly never "prove" the efficacy of the medium!) Some forty or fifty years after their introduction into schools, many people still see audiovisual materials as "frills." While the impact of the electronic mass media on our lives is evident to all, there is, indeed, less evidence for the effect of audiovisual media on the educational system.

It may be that the true abode of electronic media is outside the school room. That is the position taken by a 1960s open-education advocate, Neil Postman, who, now taking a "revisionist" stance, calls for tightly structured "linguistically centered" schools to counteract television's fragmented "image-centered" message. But media, in fact, never did replace the textbook. A 1977 Educational Products Information Exchange (EPIE) survey found 20% of responding teachers to be without instructional materials other than the text. Ninety-five percent of classroom time was associated with textbook use, according to another study the same year. The educational community as a whole is not as enamored of audiovisuals as the public's perception would have it—particularly the perception of audiovisuals' critics. Calls for "mainstreaming" the media are still heard in media center literature. The higher education journal, *Change*, not too long ago looked at media on the college campus, contrasting traditional classroom lectures with residence halls reverberating with stereo sound. It found that though each campus had a media center, its impact on academic life was generally slight.

The case for the use of audiovisuals in the classroom rests to a large extent on logical, not empirical, grounds. These include, in Lillian Wehmeyer's summary:

1. content (cannot be learned verbally);
2. nature of learning task (skills that cannot be learned verbally);
3. teaching situation (large group instruction);

4. learner preference and characteristics;
5. motivational power of media;
6. study of media as form of communication and of aesthetic experience.

Research studies of the efficacy of audiovisual media are inconclusive (for a summary of such research see *The Encyclopaedia of Educational Media Communications and Technology*).

The need for schools to equip students for life in a mass media world by teaching "media literacy" is a recognized goal; so should be the need for "visual literacy," the ability to comprehend and to express oneself in terms of visual stimuli, such as symbols, pictures, and graphics. Every teacher knows that one child may best remember what is heard, another what is seen, another what is touched, yet another what is actively experienced.

On the question of content, small audiovisual media can be produced relatively quickly, certainly more quickly than hardcover books, particularly textbooks. Five years is considered the longest period a social studies or science text should be used. Audiovisual media make it possible to update the text during those five years.

Perhaps educators have at times had unrealistic expectations of what media could accomplish within the schools' tradition-bound structure. Perhaps we used the media too casually, or perhaps we succumbed to extravagant promises and fancy packaging and bought media without a clear idea of their intended function within the instructional process. Certainly educators have been too willing to buy programs that fall far short of the media's potential: a complete enveloping of the listener/ viewer with stimuli of sight and sound that compels absorption of the desired content. We are daily exposed to this in television commercials. Evidently the talent that goes into their production has not gone into the production of instructional media. Promotion of expensive multi-image presentations of unproven instructional value and of ever more expensive gadgetry is not the answer or the way to prove the validity of mediated learning.

Pragmatically, audiovisual media are not likely to disappear from schools as long as producers keep producing and distributors keep marketing them. Proven or not, audiovisual is with us, and the marketplace calls for intelligent consumerism. Small audiovisual budgets may be a blessing in disguise if they force educators to spend more judiciously.

REFERENCES

The Encyclopaedia of Educational Media Communications and Technology. Derick Unwin and Ray McAleese, eds. Greenwood Press, 1978. 800p.

Postman, Neil. *Teaching as a Conserving Activity*. Dell, 1980. 244p.

Wehmeyer, Lillian. "Media and Learning: Present and Future," *Catholic Library World*, v. 50, November 1978, pp. 150-52; December 1978, pp. 205-211.

Media Selection — The Reality

Existing selection procedures may be among the factors causing the second-class status of audiovisual teaching materials. Audiovisual collections have been described as "a closetful of disappointing, dust-collecting items" because "these secondary purchases usually are made without the benefit of a thoughtful reviewing process" (Raskin).

The 1980-1981 president of the American Association of School Librarians (AASL) termed the "casual and undisciplined" selection of instructional materials a "scandal" in the same talk in which he expressed hope the media could finally be "mainstreamed" (Baker). Others within the profession have made similar remarks.

There is danger that microcomputer software may be selected equally as casually and with no better results. There are many comments that commercial software is of poor quality, yet educators have few efficient means to be well informed.

Erickson clearly delineated the relationship between selection by teachers for specific instructional purposes and media center selection in anticipation of specific needs. Librarians are apt to call the latter "collection development."

> Two levels of selection should be identified. The first is at the classroom teaching level. At this level the teacher selects from local or remote sources for a forthcoming unit and carries out an appropriate pre-use examination. The second level of selection is the system-wide, central distribution level. At this level the director of instructional media services must assume responsibility for selection of the best materials that teachers need to carry on their work effectively. The best basis for selection of materials at both levels is their probable contribution to valid teaching purposes (these of course being the best possible estimates of pupil needs), their excellence in technical quality, and their suitability for known groups of learners. The only valid reason for selection at the second level is to facilitate selection at the first. (*Administering Instructional Media Programs*, Macmillan, 1968).

In this text, "media selection" is used, as defined by the ERIC *Thesaurus of Descriptors*, to mean "choice of the most appropriate material or channel of communication."

Several factors may account for the present state of media selection:

1. Educators have had little practical help with purposeful selection. Standard texts on audiovisual teaching will state that medium should match objective, but neither they nor most texts on media center operation offer much concrete advice to the teacher or media director who truly wishes to follow this rule. In many texts, the term "selection" does not even appear in the index.

2. "There are no entirely satisfactory bibliographies for all nonprint materials" (Katz, p. 78). The audiovisual field has not had the benefit of the kind of easy, wide access that *Books in Print* brings to even the smallest library or bookstore. The November 1979 White House Conference on Library and Information Services resolved in favor of "multi-type library and information networks . . . . to include . . . the concept of a national lending library for print and nonprint materials" (Resolution C-2). Ambitious computerized databases have been the subject of high-level planning but are not near implementation. The result is that when it is time to order audiovisual materials, teachers and media specialists typically take to scanning a few familiar catalogs in more or less random fashion.

3. Much audiovisual purchasing in schools is done by personnel lacking librarians' training in materials selection. In 1978, library/media centers in U.S. public schools reported spending some $68 million on audiovisual supplies and materials while industry reported total elementary/high school sales of $239 million—over triple the earlier amount. And library/media centers are by no means universally staffed by persons trained in or very knowledgeable about the art and science of selection. Statistics show only 50% of elementary schools with professionally trained personnel in their media centers.

A 1979 EPIE study found that fewer than 5% of teacher training institutions surveyed offered courses in the selection of teaching materials. Master's degree programs in instructional technology do not, as a rule, require a course in selection; many do not even offer one.

Library/media specialists may feel, rightfully, that teachers need only consult them to achieve better selection; but in these days of staff cuts, there may not be enough media specialists around. The ones that are still employed are kept busy with monitoring, housekeeping, and recordkeeping duties that press for immediate attention, leaving little time for thorough searches.

4. Media examination or selection centers have been recommended for many years but have never gotten much past the proposal stage. Those that are in existence are sometimes run at the whim of distributors' largesse and developed by default.

5. *Evaluative* or learner verification data are hard to come by. Reviewers and preview examination forms generally *analyze* materials in relation to criteria such as those detailed in chapter 5, with a view to collection development. When it comes to selecting for classroom use, what is wanted is empirical data that support instructional effectiveness. (I am indebted to Jane Terwillegar for articulating this distinction.) If selection is to follow Erickson's principle (quoted on page 19) evaluation must have a place along with analysis.

6. Inventory control for audiovisual items in many schools lags behind that for books. Not knowing what is already at hand may lead to purchases of materials that duplicate or nearly duplicate other items already in the school's possession, when perhaps a different format or materials for a different ability group would have made a more valuable contribution.

College instructors have enumerated the problems they encounter with audiovisual instruction, pointing first to the difficulty of locating materials and their own lack of awareness of the functions of instructional resource centers, but also (and the relation seems clear) to the unsystematic fashion in which purchases are undertaken.

In a few years, there may be better selection aids and computerized, or at least easy bibliographic, access for media. In the meantime, instructors and media personnel in over 100,000 individual schools, over 15,000 school districts, and in colleges must make do with what they have. They must grapple with the most efficient way to spend their few remaining audiovisual dollars.

Performance budgeting requires statements of goals, of expected benefits, and of alternative courses for each budget request. Zero-based budgeting procedures, where such are instituted, are even more searching in analyzing each request for funds and in requiring performance audits. Whether educators work under such strictures or not, a materials selection system is needed to implement educational plans and to deliver function and cost-effectiveness.

REFERENCES

Baker, D. Philip. "Establishing Criteria for Evaluating Program." In *Issues in Media Management 1979*, pp. 17-26. ED 178 058.

Katz, William A. *Introduction to Reference Work*. McGraw Hill, 1978, v. I.

Raskin, Bruce. "A-V Awards." *Learning*, v. 7, December 1978, pp. 88-100.

3

Media and Instructional Development

Instructional development is "a systematic approach to the design, production, evaluation, and utilization of complete systems of instruction" (Association for Educational Communications and Technology). As that definition implies, instructional design is one part of that process, namely "the generation of specifications for learning resources/instructional system components" (*Ibid.*).

Instructional development takes place wherever learning occurs; the process was in effect long before the term was coined. Understanding the principles of ID should result in their more skillful application and in instruction pointed at more clearly defined objectives. It should result in "sharper tools for better learning," yet not stifle student creativity and the humanist dimension in education.

A system based on learners' potential and needs, ID starts with where the students are (entry behavior), defines their destination (instructional objective), and determines how to get them there and what materials to use in the process (learning strategy). Continual evaluation and assessment are essential aspects. It builds on analysis of the learning process that divides the realm of learning into the cognitive, the affective, and the motor skills. Objectives and strategies are derived from one or more of the categories delineated in the *Taxonomy of Educational Objectives* and the *Taxonomy of the Psychomotor Domain* (Harrow). Thus cognitive objectives involve knowledge, its recall, comprehension, and application, and the analysis, synthesis and evaluation of information. Affective objectives pertain to awareness of values, responding to them, valuing them, and organizing a value system and controlling one's actions accordingly. Psychomotor domain objectives are classified as reflex movements, basic movements, perceptual abilities, physical abilities, skilled movements, and nondiscursive communication, i.e., aesthetic or creative expression in movement.

Objectives state the desired behavior, the conditions under which it is to occur, and the level of mastery. Well-written objectives avoid verbs open to varying interpretations, preferring specific ones such as "compares," "constructs," "contrasts," "hits," "jumps," "lists," "names," "runs," "solves," "writes," etc.–they describe the criterion level in terms that are subject to measuring and testing. Clearly, objectives in the affective domain lend themselves less readily to such measurement and precision.

Entry behavior is also analyzed as to its cognitive, motor, and affective aspects. Verbal ability or reading comprehension relate to cognitive behavior, while attitude to school, a subject, or to one's own adequacy are examples of affective behaviors.

Measurement of students' entry competencies provide the basis for setting objectives within the confines of goals generally established outside the classroom (by the state legislature, school board, or superintendent). Goals and objectives differ

22

in their level of specificity (e.g., "punctuates sentences correctly" is a goal; "uses question marks when needed" an objective). The teacher—in this context the term "classroom strategist" has been applied—sets objectives sequentially.

A more recent formulation of educational objectives (Steinaker), fusing cognitive and affective factors, would have learning experiences follow this sequence: exposure (consciousness of an experience), participation (decision to become physically a part of an experience), identification (coming together of the learner and the objective in an emotional and intellectual context for the achievement of the objective), internalization (experience affects lifestyle of participant), and, finally, dissemination (sharing with others).

SOURCES FOR OBJECTIVES

Teachers' editions of texts, teachers' guides, and similar professional sources generally furnish statements of objectives that may be adapted to particular classroom situations. "Students should be able to identify the characteristics of reptiles and list the four groups of animals that are reptiles" is such a statement from an instructional television program (*Discovering*. Agency for Instructional Television, 1978). "The student will be able to . . . . . list the five basic areas of a window display; list the six principles for an effective display" is another example from a filmstrip program (*How to Create Effective Window Displays*. Fairchild Visuals, 1979).

Where the guide states program objectives (in reality nothing more than the subject of the program, (e.g., "to acquaint students with the components of the four stroke internal combustion engine"), the teacher must specify behavior to be attained. For the example cited, this might read "can name the strokes of the four-cycle internal combustion engine." This must also be done where program objectives are stated in terms of students' learning: The teacher showing a film whose stated objective is "to make students aware of the cruel prejudices which the Chinese immigrants faced" (*Jung Sai: Chinese American*. Macmillan, 1977) may expect students, after viewing, to be able to "name three laws that were expressions of anti-Chinese prejudice."

Teachers' guides supplied with audiovisual programs vary widely in content and quality. Some state no objective at all, though they may be excellent in other respects. What to look for in a teachers' guide is more fully discussed in chapter 5 (pp. 35-37).

LEARNING STRATEGIES

Choice of a learning strategy is a function of content, teacher knowledge of learners and their characteristics, and judgment as to optimum learning conditions. The setting and appropriate classroom organization must be chosen: lecture, class discussion, panel discussion, team activity, role playing, writing, show and tell, art work, or case study. Learning strategy also involves determining needed stimuli so that learning materials and activities for each instructional event may be chosen accordingly.

MEDIA TAXONOMIES AND USES*

The relation of media attributes and formats to specific instructional uses is the subject of much academic research, none of it as lucid as John Chancellor's observation that "television is good at the transmission of experiences, print is better at the transmission of facts" (*Time*, v. 115, February 25, 1980, p. 71). The late Justice Douglas, reminding us that all forms of expression are equally protected by the First Amendment, observed that

> on occasion one may be more powerful or effective than another. The movie, like public speech, radio, or television, is transitory—here now, and gone in an instant. The novel, the short story, the poem in printed form are permanently at hand to re-enact the drama or retell the story over and again. Which medium will give the most excitement and have the most enduring effect will vary with the theme and the actors. (346 US 587, 589).

It is possible to find support in the literature both for the proposition that certain attributes are uniquely suited to certain purposes and for the idea that media are almost interchangeable. It should be remembered that attribute is the determining factor, although research often focuses on format (a film that is a series of stills lacks motion, though it is classified as "motion picture film"; special effects can simulate motion with overhead transparencies, normally a "still-visual" format).

Media may be classified on the basis of attributes, such as:
- audio
- printed
- audio-print
- projected still-visual
- audio projected still-visual
- motion-visual
- audio-motion-visual   (Bretz)

The degree of abstraction present is another way to group media:
- direct experience
- simulation
- exhibit
- motion pictures
- still pictures
- visual word symbols
- spoken word   (Bergeson)

This classification appears to be derived from Dale's formulation which ranked experiences from the most concrete to the most abstract as follows (usually presented as Dale's "Cone of Experience):
- direct purposeful experiences
- contrived experiences
- dramatized experiences

---

*Portions of this section previously appeared in the author's contributions to *Children's House*, v. 10, Spring 1978, and *Educational Technology*, v. 19, March 1979.

- demonstration
- study trips
- exhibits
- educational television
- motion pictures
- recordings, radio, still pictures
- visual symbols
- verbal symbols

A grouping that employs common terminology and is based on needed equipment is practical:

- photographic print
- slides
- filmstrips
- recordings
- overhead transparencies
- motion pictures
- video
- multi-image/multimedia   (Kemp)

The Annehurst Curriculum Classification System recognizes ten categories:

- filmstrip, slides, films, filmloops, video
- records, audiotapes
- transparencies
- worksheets, dittos
- books, magazines, pamphlets, tests
- study prints, posters, pictures, maps, charts
- field trips
- games, flashcards, kits, activity cards, simulations
- globes, models, realia, equipment
- people.

Though the old saying tells us that "a picture is worth a thousand words," interestingly enough some studies find the verbal component to be an important factor in the effectiveness of visuals (*The Encyclopaedia of Educational Media Communications and Technology*, pp. 51, 54).

Media won't hold students' interest very long if used for no apparent reason. The single most operative word in mediated instruction should be "why?" That simple question should be asked—and honestly answered—*before* purchase and *before* classroom use. For instance: One of the best reasons for visuals is undoubtedly to give students some acquaintance with the unfamiliar. In the area of career education, for example, workbook-and-cassette units are on the market that will drill the student in test-taking or interviewing skills. Most teachers can readily devise such drills. With limited funds for audiovisual purchases, it would seem far wiser to spend money on visuals that can bring close the remote and unknown world of work and permit a glance at occupations known only by name.

The media specialist should beware of high-technology packages sold for remedial "basic skills" instruction. Some of these programs merely show on the screen what already troubles students on paper. Much less expensive games to teach computation or sentence structure, and read-along cassettes to make reading less forbidding, could be much better buys.

In the real world, one can only buy media for which one has the necessary projection equipment—no matter what the research says. The following discussion mentions some realistic observations on "appropriate technology."

Moving picture film and video are the formats of choice for affective strategies, but recorded speeches and dramatizations, musical recordings, subjective visuals, sound, and color have their affective functions, too. Where controversial subjects are involved, it may be necessary to present opposing points of view, format for format. A sober book presenting viewpoint A can hardly be said to be a proper balance to a tendentious film of the opposite persuasion. Films can successfully introduce or summarize a unit of study or a major, complex topic. Recording on video formats reduces their cost, increases their availability, and makes it easier to stop at or return to a given frame.

Filmloops are excellent for demonstrations of motor skills and of processes in nature and art.

Still pictures promote cognitive learning. The size of the group will dictate whether study prints, or projected ones, such as slides or filmstrips, are indicated. Overhead transparencies cannot achieve the realism of photographic slides but are easier and less expensive to produce. They are a popular locally produced format.

Slides may be preferred over filmstrips because they are easier to update—but it is also easier to lose single ones or to disturb their sequence.

Concrete, iconic representations promote cognitive learning. Media employing higher levels of abstraction are for learners of analytical bent.

Audiocassettes, the least expensive of the media, enjoy extensive use. They are also the most abstract. Audio and video taping are excellent for learner feedback.

Simulation games are fine in the affective realm and in developing interpersonal competencies. Simulations may be employed for purposes of intergroup rather than interpersonal academic competition (Dukes). They offer "learning by doing" (Heyman).

Realia, models, and "touch-me" exhibits are for the student with tactile orientation; media with a visual component are for the visually inclined. Color is not always a necessity. Black-and-white can convey great social realism and effectively disclose structure of natural and man-made objects. Dazzling multimedia and multi-image presentations may be confusing rather than instructive to elementary students. Choose less expensive media when either of two or more formats will do the job.

Bock's chart, "Cost-effectiveness Factors in the Media Selection Process," rates formats on their cost per student, ease of replacing, flexibility, and overall cost-effectiveness, among other factors. It finds some of the low-cost media (still visuals, cassettes) also low in overall cost-effectiveness compared to audio-motion-visual. Changes in price and salary levels may change those factors.

It is clear that the media selector must be free of preference for any one medium and must regard audiovisual materials as instructional components to be used for their unique capabilities. The end result of the selection process should be "the medium that provides:

* the greatest amount of learning
* the most desirable kinds of learning
* for the largest number of learners
* utilization over the longest period of time with minimum amount of logistical support"   (Sleeman)

To identify such media, the media center director needs to be acquainted with the principles of instructional development which guide teachers in classroom instruction and in making assignments.

The decision whether to use a ready-made program or to produce one locally, possibly having students involved in the production, reflects the chosen learning strategy.

ROLE OF THE MEDIA SPECIALIST

The teacher chooses the desired medium (and content) and expects the media center to supply what is needed (other than paper-pencil-chalkboard type of supplies). As an information manager, the media specialist must be prepared with a collection from which suitable selections can be made. The media specialist can also offer a wider knowledge of resources and can make teachers aware of the range of possibilities in both ready-made and locally manufactured products applicable to the desired learning strategy, along with the alternatives that equally meet desired criteria of stimuli and levels of abstraction. For instance, the need for a picture of a past news event can be met with a magazine clipping or a recorded television program. A transparency or slide could be made from a political cartoon (projected still visuals are first choice for in-school production). If aural representation can be substituted, the media specialist may know of a source for obtaining a cassette of a broadcast.

The teacher who becomes aware of the full range of possible learning materials can steer students to those most suitable to their capacities, learning styles, and appropriate learning objectives. A learner's achievement is monitored in relation to cost, time, and effort; the prescription of alternative strategies or materials, including ones lower in cost, and changed group size, differentiated staffing, or other changes may be indicated.

To give such help to teachers, media specialists must know the curriculum and goals of the school(s) served by a particular media center. Goals and objectives are stated in adopted curricula, curriculum guides, texts, instructional programs, and the like. It behooves the media specialist to be acquainted with these materials and to maintain up-to-date copies in the center's professional collection. Collection development in the media center that would provide underpinning for the curriculum will build on such knowledge.

It might be noted that the "ability to develop criteria and establish the correct medium for the objective or course" is among the skills the American Association of School Librarians (AASL) expects of candidates for professional school library media personnel.

MEDIA DECISIONS

Administrative considerations, such as space, teacher and principal preference, availability of equipment, and scheduling, play an important role in media decisions. In actual practice, administrative considerations may more often come first rather than last in the selection process. It would obviously be foolish for the media specialist to order audiovisual titles for which the school does not own the required projection equipment. On the other hand, if pedagogic reasons dictate—and budget permits—the purchase of a new type of projector, it would be equally foolish *not* to order programs designed for it (see also page 44).

To place budgetary considerations first may result in more pointed choices. Only by planning ahead of time for a distribution among subject area can the media center give to each subject the support it needs.

Average prices for nonprint media increased by 20% for audiocassettes and 81% for multimedia kits (Walch, David B., "Price Index for Nonprint Media," *Library Journal*, v. 106, February 15, 1981, pp. 432-33)–a clear imperative for careful budgeting.

The checklist given in figure 1 comprises all the factors, pedagogic and administrative, that go into goal-oriented media selection.

FIGURE 1–SELECTION CHECKLIST

Format
    print   motion
    audio   color
    audio-print   fixed sequence
    still-visual   referability
    projected still-visual   pacing
    audio projected still-visual
    motion-visual
    audio-motion-visual
Group size
    class
    small group
    individual
Place
    classroom
    media center
Objective
    Nature
        cognitive
            abstract
            concrete
        affective
        motor
    Level of acquisition
    Range of acquisition
        basic
        intermediate
        advanced
        mastery
Learner characteristics
    instructional level
    chronological age
    mental age
    learning style
        visual   deductive/inductive
        tactile   experiential
        auditory   verbal
        inner-directed
        quantitative
        theoretical
Teacher characteristics
Place
Time
Equipment needed

REFERENCES

Association for Educational Communications and Technology. *Educational Technology: Definition and Glossary of Terms*, 1977.

Bergeson, John. *Media in Instruction and Management Manual*. Mt. Pleasant, MI: Central Michigan University, 1976. ED 126 916.

Bretz, Rudy. *A Taxonomy of Communication Media*. Educational Technology, 1971. 168p.

Bock, D. Joleen. *The Learning Resources Center*. LJ Report No. 3. Bowker, 1977. 64p.

Dukes, Richard, ed. *Learning with Simulations and Games*. Sage, 1978.

Frymier, Jack. *Annehurst Curriculum Classification System: A Practical Way to Individualize Instruction*. West Lafayette, IN: Kappa Delta Pi, 1977. 391p.

Harrow, A. J. *Taxonomy of the Psychomotor Domain*. McKay, 1972. 190p.

Heyman, Mark. *Simulation Games for the Classroom*. Phi Delta Kappa, 1975.

Kemp, Jerrold E. *Planning and Producing Audiovisual Materials*. 4th ed. Harper, 1980.

Sleeman, Philip J. *Instructional Media and Technology*. Longman, 1979. 374p.

Steinaker, Norman W. *The Experiential Taxonomy: A New Approach to Teaching and Learning*. Academic Press, 1979. 198p.

Taxonomy of Educational Objectives; The Classification of Educational Goals. Handbook I: Cognitive Domain. Benjamin S. Bloom, ed. McKay, 1956. 207p.

Taxonomy of Educational Objectives; The Classification of Educational Goals. Handbook II: Affective Domain. David R. Kratwohl, et al., eds. McKay, 1964. 196p.

Individualized Instruction

Instructional development principles apply to large or small groups of students or to individuals; they can refer to planning a lesson or an entire curriculum. When ID is employed with the aim of individualizing instruction, students' learning characteristics and styles become prime determinants. Individualization may affect choice of instructional objectives, strategies, materials and activities, and pacing of the lesson(s).

The teacher can build individualization into each class period and each assignment, or elect one of the formalized structures known by acronyms such as IPI (Individually Prescribed Instruction), IGE (Individually Guided Education), PIC (Process Individualized Curriculum), or PSI (Personalized System of Instruction). Individual learning contracts are a favorite device. Whatever method, precision in media selection is a necessity. Since frequent monitoring of student progress is a common feature of individualized learning strategies, media prescriptions can be adjusted as indicated by such feedback.

Learning activity packages (LAP) are commonly used devices for implementing individualized instruction. They almost always state the objectives the student is to attain (and to what extent), and provide a pretest based on these objectives, before detailing the readings, activities, and other assignments the student is to complete before taking the post-test.

Individualized Educational Plans (IEP) are required by law for all handicapped children. The IEP is expected to state present performance, annual goals, short-term instructional objectives, participation in special programs and in regular classrooms, and evaluation procedures. This requirement of the Education for All Handicapped Children Act (P.L. 94-142) has caused the special education community to pay special attention to careful selection and evaluation of learning materials. The criteria turn out to be not all that different from those applicable to materials for other students.

At the other end of the spectrum, gifted students can also benefit from individualization which recognizes and takes into account their intellectual or creative talents. Gifted and talented students need to be held to intellectually demanding content and processes, whether the output of the learning experience be in written or media format.

The Annehurst Curriculum Classification System owes its origin to a desire to match characteristics of subject matter and of learning materials to those of learners. The latter are defined in ten categories:

> experiential
> intellectual
> motivational
> emotional person
> creativity

    social

    verbal expression

    auditory expression

    visual expression

    motor perception

The literature cited below offer additional observations:

Anderson, Robert M., et al. *Individualizing Educational Materials for Special Children in the Mainstream*. Baltimore: University Park Press, 1978. 393p.

Baskin, Barbara H., and Harris, Karen H. *Books for the Gifted Child*. Bowker, 1980. 263p.

Duane, James E. "What Media Should Be Used to Individualize Instruction?" *Journal of Personalized Instruction*, v. 3, Fall 1978, pp. 168-70.

Frymier, Jack. *The Annehurst Curriculum Classification System*. 1977.

Gartner, Alan, and Riessman, Frank. *How to Individualize Learning*. (Fastback #100). Phi Delta Kappa, 1977. 29p.

Jobe, Holly. *Creating the Learning Activities Package*. 1975. ED 171 311.

Jobe, Holly. *Producing Learning Activities Packages; Instructor's Manual*. 1978. ED 171 322.

Langrehr, John. "Match the Materials and the Learners," *Audiovisual Instruction*, v. 23, September 1978, pp. 19-22.

Smith, Janice. "Media Services for Gifted Students: An Overview." *School Media Quarterly*, v. 8, Spring 1980, pp. 161-68, 177-78.

Woodbury, Marda. *Selecting Materials for Instruction; Issues and Policies*. Libraries Unlimited, 1979. "Selecting 'Individualized' Materials," pp. 272-92; "Selecting for Gifted Education," pp. 333-42.

Selection Guidelines and Criteria

Guidelines and performance criteria issued by state education departments direct media specialists in the operation of media centers, including the selection of materials. Additional direction is received from regional accrediting agencies and national organizations such as the National Education Association, American Association of School Librarians, Association for Educational Communications and Technology, Educational Products Information Exchange, and others. Those in the last category express the aspirations and highest standards of the profession. They achieve implementation to the extent they are incorporated in the more binding rules of state and regional evaluators.

It should be noted that all documents discussed in this chapter apply to all forms of instructional materials—textbooks, trade books, reference books, etc., as well as audiovisual media. Few of these documents speak to the kind of goal-oriented selection that is the subject of the present work. Indiana's *Guidelines for Indiana School Media Programs* may come closest:

> "The primary focus of the media collection should be on curriculum-related materials. Teachers must find the resources to meet the demands of their instructional methods and teaching style" (p. 6).

Nor do many—if any—of them relate the selection process to the cost of an item. Among writers on media selection, Bruce is one of the few who does so, advising that selection be done directly from vendor catalogs for inexpensive items and that previewing only be done for expensive ones. It would seem self-evident that it does not pay to spend more on the selection process (counting staff time and resources) than the cost of the item under consideration. Bruce does not further define "inexpensive." That definition clearly changes with the general price level, but probably should be predetermined, possibly on a per capita basis, taking account of the fact that audiovisuals generally are used in group rather than individual situations.

STATE GUIDELINES AND PERFORMANCE CRITERIA

To receive federal funds under the Elementary and Secondary Education Act, Title IV-B, schools must meet specific standards, and state education departments must in turn promulgate appropriate rules. These deal, among other topics, with the selection of materials. That such selection must proceed in accordance with clearly stated criteria is a requirement, and states have adopted varying lists of such criteria. Nebraska's may be unique in recommending the exact subject distribution (by percentages in each Dewey Decimal classification) of secondary school library books (*Regulations and Procedures for the Accreditation of Public and Non-Public Schools*, p. 23).

Besides enumerating such desirable qualities as authority, lack of bias, appropriate presentation and sequencing, and the like, some states directly address the instructional utility of materials, thus expecting a true evaluation rather than analysis of them (e.g., Washington's *ESEA Title IV-b Handbook*, pp. 8-9). Several of the states stress the need for weeding out obsolete and inappropriate materials.

Because of the wide diversity of state-adopted criteria, the compilation on page 34 only tabulates those of national agencies.

Other portions of state guidelines generally address the purposes which media center collections are to serve (curricular, but often also noncurricular), participants in the selection process, general procedures, procedures for controversial materials, and the need for an adopted selection policy. Model selection policies may be supplied, again with statements of criteria, goals, procedures, etc. Having such a policy on the books can strengthen a school's position when would-be censors start to question purchases.

Teachers are expected to participate in materials selection according to the rules and regulations of several states. Some documents clearly state that department heads have final responsibility for choosing texts, while media specialists decide on all other instructional materials. Student participation is encouraged in some jurisdictions, and several states are rather emphatic in involving "community persons" in the selection process, particularly when challenged materials are to be reviewed.

Parenthetically, a provision for teacher input into instructional materials selection is a common provision in teacher contracts. Despite this contractual right and administrative direction in many jurisdictions, teachers do very little of this, if an EPIE survey is to be believed. It found 45% of classroom teachers surveyed stating they had no such role. The 54% who did, spent one hour per year on it, or less!

NATIONAL GUIDELINES AND STANDARDS

The guidelines on selection from various national professional organizations vary in emphasis and in approach, depending on whether they are addressed primarily to classroom teachers, media specialists, special education personnel, or parents. They also show extensive agreement, as the table which follows shows. The criteria issued by educators' groups address evaluation of instructional effectiveness more than do those of the American Association of School Librarians. Those in turn provide for deeper analysis of quality. (See figure 2, page 34.)

SPECIFIC FORMATS

Woodbury's *Selecting Materials for Instruction: Media and the Curriculum* deals exhaustively with special considerations that may be applicable to specific formats. It devotes separate chapters to games and simulations, pictorial media, toys and other manipulatives, among others.

FIGURE 2—SELECTION CRITERIA OF LEADING PROFESSIONAL ORGANIZATIONS

	NEA	AASL	AECT	EPIE	Brown	NCEMMH
Content						
Authority	x	x		x		
Accuracy	x		x		x	x
Currency	x	x			x	
Objectivity			x			
Sequence & arrangement	x			x		x
Scope				x		
Curriculum-related	x	x			x	x
Instructional level		x	x	x	x	x
Learner characteristics	x	x	x	x		x
Adapted to self-instru.	x					x
Stimul. creativity		x				
Pluralistic	x	x				
Rel. to personal stud. needs		x	x			x
Aesthetic & ethical values		x	x			
Treatment of controversial subjects		x	x			
Technical quality	x	x				x
Graphics		x				x
Picture		x			x	x
Sound		x			x	x
Sound/picture integrity		x				
Editing						
Packaging						x
Format appr. to message					x	
Clarity, readability		x	x			
Methodology						
State instr. objectives				x		x
Sequential progress	x					x
Size of group				x		
Evaluation				x	x	x
Teacher style				x		x
Point of View		x	x			
Bias-free			x			
Relevant	x	x				
Student self-image & devel.		x	x			
Ancillary materials						
Teacher's guide	x					x
Learner verification				x		x
Validation supplied				x	x	
Administrative Factors						
Time				x		x
Space				x		
Staff				x		x
Cost	x			x	x	x

National Education Association. *Instructional Materials: Selection and Purchase.* Rev. ed. 1976. ED 130 380.

American Association of School Librarians. *Policies and Procedures for Selection of Instructional Materials.* 1976.

Association for Educational Communications and Technology. *Media, the Learner, and Intellectual Freedom.* 1979.

Educational Products Information Exchange. *Improving Materials Selection Procedures: A Basic "How To" Handbook* (Report No. 54). 1973.

Brown, James W. *Administering Educational Media.* McGraw-Hill, 1977.

National Center on Educational Media and Materials for the Handicapped. *Standard Criteria for the Selection and Evaluation of Instructional Material* (1976).

SPECIFIC SUBJECTS

Criteria for materials dealing with specific subjects take note of the peculiar ways in which that subject may have been misrepresented. Examples are the Textbook Evaluation Guidelines of the Asia Society, the Media Evaluation Checklist of the African Studies Center at Michigan State University, *Criteria for Selecting Instructional Materials for Nutrition Education*, and guidelines for materials for business education (Dlabay) and gerontology (Davis). The *Nutrition* materials criteria—warning to watch out for fad words and phrases and for pictures and language that can quickly date materials—can be heeded in selecting materials for other subjects as well.

Evaluation forms devised for use in special education and in the preparation of IEP's (see page 30) emphasize learner characteristics, as may be expected, and generally pay greater attention to methodology than do general purpose lists of criteria.

TEACHERS' GUIDES

The quality of a teacher's guide—and whether one is provided at all—can often mean the difference between a program's continuous and active use and its sitting in the closet. Despite this fact, teachers' guides are not infrequently omitted from consideration in criteria checklists. Figures 3A (page 36) and 3B (page 37) include an 11-point teacher guide evaluation with definitions. Though intended for film and television, it is equally applicable to guides supplied with other formats. Reproductions of visuals and pre- and post-tests are additional desirable features. Certainly an exceptional guide can be expected to accompany a high-priced program.

Ideally, the materials selected for instructional development will come from those that fit stated criteria. The sheer mass of criteria from so many different sources may seem overwhelming. With some practice, the selector quickly develops the requisite confidence and judgment in their application, however.

FIGURE 3A—TEACHER GUIDE EVALUATION*

TEACHER GUIDE EVALUATION

Circle the response you judge appropriate, based on the definitions.

1.	FORMAT	YES	NO	
2.	TABLE OF CONTENTS	YES	NO	
3.	LEARNING OBJECTIVES	YES	NO	
4.	VIDEO SUMMARY	YES	NO	
5.	VOCABULARY	YES	NO	NA
6.	STUDENT MATERIALS	YES	NO	NA
7.	PRE-VIEWING	YES	NO	
8.	POST-VIEWING	YES	NO	
9.	BIBLIOGRAPHY	YES	NO	
10.	RELEVANCE	YES	NO	
11.	MOTIVATION	YES	NO	

Additional comments:

*Reprinted from *Guidelines for Evaluating Instructional Media*, State Department of Education, Juneau, Alaska, 1978.

FIGURE 3B—TEACHER GUIDE EVALUATION—DEFINITIONS*

DEFINITIONS

CRITERIA FOR EVALUATING INSTRUCTIONAL MEDIA

TEACHER GUIDE

1. **Format**
   Attractive and easy to follow; print legible; graphics or photos clear.

2. **Table of Contents**
   Contains table of contents giving clear outline of guide; contents well-organized.

3. **Learning Objectives**
   Stated for each program; adequate for determining expected types of learning or performance outcomes.

4. **Video Summary**
   Summary of video program content provided for each program. Provides adequate information for determining type of presentation(s) contained in program, and specific program events requiring student viewer prep.

5. **Vocabulary**
   Technical terms are listed and defined.

6. **Student Materials**
   All student materials are provided in format allowing easy duplicating.

7. **Pre-Viewing**
   Contains suggestions for pre-viewing classroom discussion, activities, or prep that will improve viewer readiness for viewing.

8. **Post-Viewing**
   Suggestions for post-viewing classroom discussion or activities do not simply re-teach video program content, but assist classroom follow-up to stimulate further student understanding, study, or inquiry.

9. **Bibliography**
   Includes listing of reference materials for additional or individual study.

10. **Relevance**
    Provides realistic suggestions for classroom activities to complement video program viewing; suggestions are practical and usable without extensive prep or elaborate additional materials.

11. **Motivation**
    Guide stimulates interest in using video series with accompanying classroom activities.

---

*Reprinted from *Guidelines for Evaluating Instructional Media*, State Department of Education, Juneau, Alaska, 1978.

REFERENCES

African Studies Center, Michigan State University, East Lansing, MI 48824.

Asia Society. *Asia in American Textbooks*. 1976. 36p. ED 127 232.

Bruce, Elaine. "Locating Audio-visual Materials: A North American Perspective." *International Yearbook of Educational and Instructional Technology, 1978/79.* pp. 207-214.

Davis, Richard H., and Lambert, Theresa N. "Media: Theory and Uses." In Hirschfield, Ira S., and Lambert, Theresa N. *Audio-Visual Aids: Uses & Resources in Gerontology*. Andrus Gerontology Center, University of Southern California, 1978, pp. 8-20.

Dlabay, Les R. "Basic Business Materials Identification, Evaluation, and Selection," *Business Education Forum*, v. 32, April 1978, pp. 24-26.

Moore, Inez. *Criteria for Selecting Instructional Materials for Nutrition Education.* 1979. 13p. ED 169 913.

6
Needs Assessment

It is one thing to agree that media center collections should meet the needs—curricular and possibly extracurricular—of the schools; it's quite another to ascertain what those needs are. Some writers, regional accrediting agencies, and state guidelines admonish media people and librarians to maintain "balanced collections" without specifying just how to determine "balance." A state supervisor of instructional media has observed that "the only really balanced collection is one that reflects the curricular needs of that particular school in the formats most useful to those students" (Walker).

Involving teachers, students, and parents in the selection process ideally would make their needs known to the person responsible for selection. It is difficult, in practice, to get people to express their needs. Students may not need prodding to make their wants known. Teachers, however, don't like to feel they need help, especially from someone (the library/media person) who is not a subject specialist in the teacher's own field. Yet, as the EPIE study showed, teachers do not, by and large, engage actively in media selection.

Turner's "Software Search and Verification Form," reproduced in figure 4 (page 40), recommends itself for its simplicity. State rules and regulations require other forms. The assessment must be highly specific regardless of whether such formal means or a less structured process is employed. Information that is not specific is not likely to be used.

Where state guidelines refer to needs assessment, this most often is defined in terms of meeting national or state standards. Typically, these are promulgated in measurable, quantitative terms, laced with qualitative admonitions. To find out from such a comparison that one's media center lacks x number of filmstrips of recent copyright date is very well; to pinpoint specific titles to remedy that lack requires supplementing such quantitative assessment with anecdotal data.

As has been noted on page 32, some states mandate distribution of library books among various Dewey Decimal classes. Even were this distribution to be observed for media other than books, knowing that x titles must be added to the 500s again does not specify which titles or for which ability levels. Woodbury's "Library or Media Collection: Assessment Chart" to some degree refines such analysis by Dewey classification, but again not to the needed level of specificity.

Checking against standard catalogs and curriculum guides is specifically required by some state guidelines, and states may supply lists of recommended selection aids (note those of Iowa and Washington) and/or of recommended media (note those of North Carolina, frequently entered in ERIC). A true assessment of needs can begin with such checking. More informal daily feedback from teachers and students, along with assembling of anecdotal data, will supplement it.

FIGURE 4—SOFTWARE SEARCH AND VERIFICATION FORM*

Software Search and Verification Form

The following form allows the teacher to state well ahead of time the objectives that will be taught. You, as the media person, can recommend either several commercially produced materials, materials already on hand, or the production of the materials by the audiovisual department.

Software search and verification form.

SOFTWARE SEARCH AND VERIFICATION FORM			
I will be covering the following topics, and would like information on the materials available.			
NAME_____DATE NEEDED_____			
TOPIC	OBJECTIVE	LEVEL	RECOMMENDATION

*Reprinted by permission of Libraries Unlimited from Turner, Philip M. *Handbook for School Media Personnel*. 2nd ed. 1980. p. 93.

Carrying out formal evaluations annually, as may be required by adopted selection policies, may be ideal. If this cannot be achieved, regular intervals should at least be the aim.

As Iowa's definition of the "selection continuum" states:

"Material is purchased to meet a need. It is reviewed and examined, if possible, prior to purchase; it is periodically reevaluated through updating, discarding, or reexamination." (p. 12).

Where formal or informal needs assessment procedures result in discarding of dated materials or materials that have otherwise lost their usefulness or no longer fit the selection criteria, a decision must be made whether to replace them. It is possible, of course, that the materials will have been on a subject no longer being taught and therefore they are not likely to be requested by students on their own volition. In other cases, a replacement for a different ability level or in a different format may be indicated.

Needs indicators include:

- inability to fill student or teacher requests
- specific teacher requests
- adoption of new curricula or basal texts
- adoption of changed teaching methods
- gaps shown up during weeding of collection
- checking against appropriate recommended lists

In each case, the media selector will pinpoint as specifically as possible:

- topic
- learning objective
- learner characteristics
- intended use (size of group, time span)
- teacher preference

The simplest way to keep abreast of one's clients' needs is to keep what may be termed a "Needs File." Only a simple form is needed, perhaps on a 5x8-inch sheet of paper, where it is possible to note specific topic, grade level, intended use or uses, preferred format, when and for how long needed, and name of the person originating the request. These "needs" will generally be by subject rather than title. A model needs assessment form is shown in figure 5 (page 42).

In compiling a needs file, a conscious effort should be made to ascertain not only the needs of present media center users but the unarticulated concerns of non-users as well. Teacher consultation is the prime way to accomplish this. Spreading the word of what the media center has to offer, personal contact and inquiry, and suggestion boxes are other recommended ongoing procedures. The introduction of a new equipment item with accompanying software can be a good attention-getter.

The needs file provides the raw materials for the selection process. It alerts the media specialist to be on the lookout for what is truly needed. Once a likely item is flagged, a card or sheet describing it can then be placed in a "Want File." Titles found in standard collections that are desired for purchase can proceed directly to that file.

A worksheet such as that illustrated in figure 6 (page 43) makes a practical form for entries in a "Want File." As data about a particular program are recorded on it, the data still missing and the sources still to be consulted are clearly revealed (specific suggestions are in the chapters that follow and the Pathfinder chart on page 54).

FIGURE 5—NEEDS ASSESSMENT FORM

SUBJECT OR TOPIC _____ BUDGETED AMOUNT _____

OBJECTIVES

Cognitive	Affective	Motor

INSTRUCTIONAL LEVEL(S) _____

STUDENT CHARACTERISTICS _____

EXPECTED USAGE   Media Center _____   Number of Students _____

                 Classroom _____   Length of Time _____

                 Date Needed _____

DESIRED ATTRIBUTES

Visual	Audio	Projection	Color	Motion

HOW ORIGINATED   Teacher _____   Administrator _____

                Student _____   Media Specialist _____

FIGURE 6—SELECTION WORKSHEET

Set	Title	Size ## of pages ## of frames	Running Time	Contents Remarks*
Segments				

Tchr's guide _____				
Producer _____		Distributor		Grade level
Release date _____		Format		Price
Source _____	Date	Page	Remarks*	
Producer _____				
Clark _____				
Ch.Ctr. _____				
SSSS _____				
Core Coll. _____				
ESLC _____				
MRD _____				
Horn _____				
SLJ _____				
Sci.Bks _____				
Booklist _____				
NICEM _____				
Other (name) _____				

Abbreviations:

Ch.Ctr.	Children's Book and Music Center
ESLC	Elementary School Library Collection
Horn	Guide to Simulations/Games
MRD	Media Review Digest
SSSS	Social Studies School Service
Sci.Bks.	Science Books and Films

*Record here quotes, references to alternative titles, other considerations for selection decisions

Copies of catalog entries and reviews can be attached to the form, which is for assembling what one wants to know about a title *before* previewing it. For the preview itself, a form that incorporates the evaluation criteria adopted by one's district, probably adapted from those recommended by various national professional organizations will be needed. (See figure 2 on page 34.) A model evaluation form is reprinted on page 47.

Making a deliberate process of needs assessment a part of the media selection process not only serves teachers and students better, but it also gives the school a stronger defense against would-be censors. Indeed, such attacks may, on occasion, be a function of media use at inappropriate maturity levels or with inadequate preparation.

REFERENCES

Walker, Nancy. In *Issues in Media Management*, 1979. p. 39. ED 178 058.

Preliminary Selection

The process described in the previous chapter and in this one goes on the entire school year, not just at budget preparation time. If handled in this way, the media specialist will always have a want list ready should funds suddenly turn up and have to be spent quickly. "Developing extensive 'consideration for purchase' files of book and nonbook media" is, it may be noted, one of the competencies expected of school librarians by the Canadian School Library Association.

Since the universe from which choices can be made is far larger than the reach of available monies, it is wise to establish parameters for the process at the outset and avoid overload. Such "criteria for elimination" will limit the field from which final selections are made, much as elimination heats limit athletic competitions. The preliminary selection process will then result in a list of titles for preview or possible purchase, limited by factors such as the following:

1. **Subject.** Whether balance among Dewey classes is prescribed by law or local policy, or is left up to the judgment of the media center director, some preliminary subject distribution must be envisioned. Knowing the total budget for audiovisuals for the year and the needs that become apparent as a result of formal collection evaluation, a budget for each curriculum area can be set (a better measure than Dewey classes since curricula cut across the latter).

2. **Format.** This is a function of all of the analysis which has gone into instructional development and of available equipment, the need to supplement rather than duplicate existing holdings, and the need to be cost-effective. The *Media Program Recommendations* of the North Carolina Department of Public Instruction state:

> "The interdependence of materials and equipment must be recognized as collections are planned and implemented. Materials in many different formats cannot be used without the appropriate equipment. Generous acquisition of these materials is paradoxically negated if the equipment needed for their use is not provided or is provided in too limited numbers. By the same reasoning, equipment can contribute to learning only if appropriate materials are available for use with that equipment" (p. 19).

3. **Cost.** An upper limit may be set for the amount to be spent per set or kit. If such a limit is set, it is astounding how many perfectly good titles can be found selling for under that amount. Some concept of "unit pricing" needs to be applied so that the amount bears some relation to the contents. For example, if a particular media center has a limit of $100 or $150, an initial judgment can be made whether it would be worth it (regardless of laudatory reviews) to spend $80 for *any* set of three audiocassettes and a 50-page booklet; or whether it is wise to spend $50 for two 25-minute cassettes, regardless of the importance of the subject. The size of the group for which the program is intended, the number of pupils likely to use it,

and its projected "life-expectancy" could help establish a per capita cost limit. Certainly, the consensus of reviewers would be considered in relation to the price of the item.

4. **Length**. An initial judgment may be made not to purchase any filmstrip under a given number of frames. Obviously, two strips of thirty-seven and forty-one frames have the same content as one with seventy-eight frames, but they cost twice as much. The shorter length may be desirable, perhaps for younger children, but the price should bear some relation to both the quality and length of the filmstrip.

5. **Teacher's guide**. A decision could be made to eliminate from consideration any program not offering a teacher's guide or which provides only a minimal one. Such programs will inevitably see less use, and less effective use, than those which have useful guides. Probably eight to twelve pages are required to meet the expectations outlined on pp. 35-37. Unfortunately, catalog descriptions generally offer no detail about guides.

6. **Utility of each component part**. If only the workbook is useful, one may reasonably question whether it is worth paying $10 for a set that also includes a gratuitous cassette. If a reliable review indicates the teacher's guide is the best part of a unit, perhaps the guide alone can be purchased or an equivalent book located.

7. **Recency**. A cut-off date should be observed, particularly for materials in science and social studies. Once that is done, there is no need to consider anything more than two years old.

Such elimination criteria need not be absolute; provision can always be made for exceptional cases.

Input for preliminary selection will come from suggestions in curriculum guides, teachers' editions of texts, reviews in professional journals, listing in the selection aids described later in this volume, previewing by staff, examination at an exhibit or examination center, and from vendor catalogs or advertising circulars. Teachers, administrators, media personnel, even students, will make nominations, each of which will be subject to rigorous scrutiny.

Distributors vary considerably in the amount of objective data they supply in their catalogs, and release dates are one of the more difficult bits of information to find on audiovisual titles, without actually seeing them. (By contrast, learning the copyright date of a book not in hand is child's play.) Since catalogs carry programs up to ten or more years old this is important to know *before* requesting a preview print. (A fuller discussion of vendors catalogs occurs on pages 121-24.)

Sales people can, of course, supply the missing data, and selectors should insist on obtaining the information.

Previewing and Reviews

PREVIEWING

Previewing prior to purchase is the unanimous admonition of textbook writers and of state and national guidelines, but it is rarely related to cost (an exception was noted on page 32 above). The recommended selection policy of the State of Washington tempers the advice slightly:

"*Whenever possible and practical*, all instructional materials under consideration for purchase shall be previewed and evaluated . . . ." (6122-5) (emphasis supplied).

In actual practice, it may be advisable to adopt a policy to preview all items costing over a given dollar amount, perhaps $25, or in some cases $50. Previewing before classroom use is always a must.

The ideal previewing situation would be where many titles on the same subject in various formats could be compared simultaneously. This is rarely possible. If this could be done, materials would more often "be selected for their strengths rather than rejected for their weaknesses," as Iowa's model selection policy advises (II.A. 7). Using good notes is the next best way of making comparisons.

An evaluation form will be an inestimable aid in achieving consistency in previewing (one is reprinted below). It can be brief:

"Comparing something against a short evaluation list and doing the same for all alternative materials is better than developing a massive screening process that you never quite get to" (Bleil, p. 20).

The evaluation form of the regrettably defunct Bay Area Media Evaluation Guild resulted in superior appraisals.

Possible additions to a form as the one shown in figure 7 might include questions about a program's adaptability to varying teaching situations, populations, and methods; unusual storage or maintenance problems; field test and learner verification data; and whether tests are included. If applicable, "ability level" may be added to "grade level."

Charging a fee for preview prints, a practice recently started by some film distributors, will, it is hoped, not spread to the distributors of smaller media. Certainly, it is only common courtesy to return preview prints promptly regardless of whether a fee is charged.

FIGURE 7—EVALUATION FORM*

BAY AREA MEDIA EVALUATION GUILD

Title: _____ Grades: _____

Producer: _____ ⊙Date: _____

_____ FS _____ RD $_____ (#   ) _____TC $_____ (#   )

Dewey No. _____ Sears Headings _____

Rating	Titles	Frames	Minutes

Contents:

CRITERIA

AUTHENTICITY	TECHNICAL	EVALUATION:
Accuracy	Artwork	
Impartiality	Photos	
Up-to-Date	Color	
Relevance	Composition	
	Audio	
APPROPRIATENESS	Vocal	
Vocabulary	Fr/Time	
Concepts	Coord	
Subject Corr.		
Curric Corr.	SPECIAL	
Ind/Gp use	Packaging	
Suited to medium	Cost	
Student appeal		
	GUIDE	
ORGANIZATION	Objectives	
Development	Background	
Scope	Summaries	
Depth	Scripts	
Sequence	Questions	
Pace	Activities	
Balance	Vocabulary	
Narration	Biblio	
Captions		

*Bay Area Media Evaluation Guild. *Evaluation Form*. Reprinted by permission.

REVIEWS

When making purchase decisions, media specialists generally are admonished to consider favorable reviews in authoritative sources only, a practice that cannot be followed in the case of audiovisual media because the percentage of those reviewed is small. For formats such as study prints, filmloops, transparencies, spoken recordings, and videocassettes the proportion is negligible.

It is ironic that there is far less consumer advice for quite costly audiovisual formats than for less expensive books. Though reviewers occasionally misunderstand a writer's intent, vent their own biases, or otherwise mislead, by and large book buying can rely on reviews. Book reviewing has, of course, a history of hundreds of years. In the case of audiovisuals, negative reviews are quite rare—leaving the reader uncertain whether an unreviewed program was deemed unworthy or simply not considered at all.

Favorable reviews may, however, take the place of previewing before purchase for less expensive items, with the number of favorable reviews scaled to the cost.

The guidelines followed by a reviewer of a journal should be known and should ideally incorporate criteria similar to those applied by school personnel in making their own evaluations. *Booklist* and *Science Books and Films* print their reviewers' instructions periodically.

Few published reviews address whether a medium is used to best advantage, make cross-media comparisons, or evaluate the quality of teachers' guides.

It should also be pointed out that what reviewers like may not be what a particular school needs. Selecting only from titles receiving favorable reviews could easily result in overrepresentation of language arts titles. For example, *Booklist* reviews more of these titles than it does, say, science works. Is it editorial choice or are the latter less frequently submitted?

One of the few articles in the literature that details a painstaking selection process for a highly specific purpose makes little mention of reviews. The reason can be surmised: what the author was looking for was not the type of material submitted to, or likely to find favor with, reviewers.

The thoughtful article by Meszaros has more to say about selecting nonfiction materials for children with reading problems than a shelfful of jargon- and acronym-studded research reports. Her efforts to compile multimedia science units on subjects popular with elementary school students revealed that there were almost no captioned sound-filmstrips or book-tape combinations on science. These children who had difficulty with printed symbols and with generalizations also had difficulty with the lush photography often employed in science filmstrips. They could handle a concise body of information on a single concept if it was illustrated with clear line drawings. Some of the materials she found successful with her students may well have been dismissed as "pedestrian" by reviewers, while 'award-winners were nothing but a source of frustration to these youngsters.

Reviews may gain in significance if vendors begin charging for preview prints. But even in the area of educational films, where reviewing is well developed, "reliance on published reviews, evaluations, awards . . . . exists more in theory than in practice," according to a knowledgeable observer (Egan).

At this writing, the prospect for extensive review coverage of audiovisual media appears unpromising and the need for better mediagraphic access greater than ever.

REFERENCES

Bleil, Gordon. "Evaluating Educational Materials." *Journal of Learning Disabilities*, v. 8, January 1975, pp. 12-19.

Egan, Catherine. "Confronting the Problem of Previewing." *Media and Methods*, v. 16, January 1980, pp. 56-59.

Meszaros, Katharine M. "The Single-Concept Approach." *School Library Journal*, v. 26, October 1979, pp. 128-29.

Final Selection

The preliminary selection process should have resulted in ample data and notes assembled by the time purchase orders are due. Now is the time for hard choices that inevitably involve compromise. Hardhearted elimination during the preliminary states will reduce the amount of compromise required; so will having ready at hand the data needed for decisionmaking about each title. The media specialist must closely examine comparable titles to identify the one that:

1) best matches with desired or stated instructional objectives;

2) offers greatest coverage in relation to cost;

3) offers availability of partial purchase (in the case of filmstrip sets);

4) includes a quality teacher's guide;

5) is up to date.

Occasionally, some components of a kit or set are valuable enough to outweigh others lacking merit. The determining factor here would be reasonable cost in relation to potential benefit and the need for subject coverage.

The next step in final selection is to make cross-media evaluations. For example, one producer markets slide and filmstrip formats of the same title through separate companies. The filmstrips are less than half the price of slide carousels. Are the advantages of the slide format sufficient to warrant the greater outlay? A film may be rented from the regional film library but is not always available when wanted. Does projected usage justify the purchase of a filmstrip set on the same subject? Would it be as effective? A filmstrip on art has exquisite visuals but the narration is dull. Would a heavily illustrated book be a better choice?

At this point, too, it may become clear that nothing on the market quite meets stated needs and that local production is indicated. Commercial media may cover too much or too little, both in content and in instructional level span. Homemade media will rarely have the same technical quality as commercial ones, but they may be more closely structured to specified instructional objectives. Though they may appear to save money, their hidden costs can be enormous since many hours of effort may be required to produce just a few minutes of program.

The policies of each district will determine when and how purchase requests are to be submitted. Only rarely does one receive everything ordered. It is smart to have a second-priority want list ready and to submit that before any funds are lost.

PART II

The process outlined in part I does not require a library full of reference books, but it does require some finesse in using a few selected tools. These are described in detail in the pages that follow, with hints on how to use them most advantageously in combination. The individual media center, unless exceptionally large or well funded, won't have all of the works on hand, but many district or regional centers and college libraries will have them available.

Selection Tools and Sources

Most of the tools described in this chapter are primarily retrospective, annotating titles released anywhere from a year to several years prior to publication. That fact alone makes those issued at annual or biennial intervals the most valuable. It goes without saying that the most recent edition should always be used, but all sources must be supplemented by keeping abreast of current production.

The selection tools and sources included here are each described separately. Figure 8, however, provides a quick overview of their grade level and format coverage, and figure 9, page 54, shows how the different types of selection aids can be used to meet common selection needs.

FIGURE 8—SCOPE OF LEADING SELECTION AIDS

elem.	sec.	college	Selection aid	Criti-cal	Current	Film-loops	Filmstrips & Kits	Pictorial mat.	Games*	Slide- (sound & silent)	Sound record-ing	Trans-parency	Video recording
x	x	x	AIT Catalog (annual)		x								x
x	x	x	Booklist (bimonthly)	x	x		x			x	x		x
x			Children's Book & Music Center (annual)		x		x	x	x	x	x		
x	x	x	Charles W. Clark Catalog (annual)		x	x	x	x		x	x	x	
x			Core Media Collection for Elementary Schools	x		x	x			x	x		
	x		Core Media Collection for Secondary Schools	x		x	x			x	x		
x			Elementary School Library Collection (biennial)	x		x	x	x	x	x	x	x	
x	x	x	GPN Catalog (annual)		x								x
	x	x	Guide to Simulations/ Games	x					x				
	x	x	Library Journal (bimonthly)**	x	x		x			x	x		x
x	x	x	Media Review Digest (annual)	x		x	x	x	x	x	x		x
x	x	x	NICEM Indexes (triennial)			x	x			x	x	x	x
x	x		School Library J. (monthly) *a	x	x		x	x		x	x		x
x	x	x	Science Books and Films	x	x		x						
x	x	x	Social Studies School Service			x	x	x	x	x	x	x	
x	x	x	Vendor Catalogs		x	x	x	x	x	x	x	x	x

* Both table games and simulations
** Annual "AV Forecast" and "AV Showcase" are not critical

FIGURE 9–PATHFINDER FOR MEDIA SELECTION

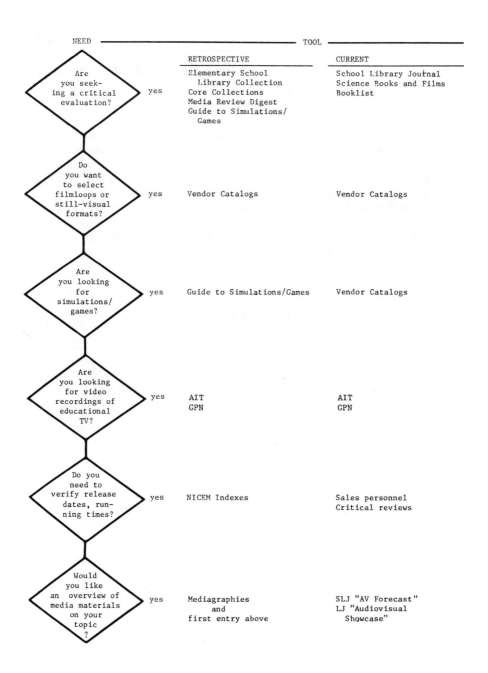

NEED		TOOL	
		RETROSPECTIVE	CURRENT
Are you seeking a critical evaluation?	yes	Elementary School Library Collection Core Collections Media Review Digest Guide to Simulations/ Games	School Library Journal Science Books and Films Booklist
Do you want to select filmloops or still-visual formats?	yes	Vendor Catalogs	Vendor Catalogs
Are you looking for simulations/ games?	yes	Guide to Simulations/Games	Vendor Catalogs
Are you looking for video recordings of educational TV?	yes	AIT GPN	AIT GPN
Do you need to verify release dates, running times?	yes	NICEM Indexes	Sales personnel Critical reviews
Would you like an overview of media materials on your topic ?	yes	Mediagraphies and first entry above	SLJ "AV Forecast" LJ "Audiovisual Showcase"

AIT CATALOG OF EDUCATIONAL MATERIALS

Agency for Instructional Television
Box A
Bloomington, IN 47402

The bulk of prepared videocassettes and other videorecordings used in education most likely will derive from two sources, the Agency for Instructional Television and the Great Plains National Instructional Television Library (see pp. 82-86). Their free catalogs should certainly be at every media director's reach. Media centers should also be on the mailing lists of these agencies to receive newsletters, announcements, and catalog supplements.

AIT was created in 1973 to provide a structure for cooperative production of televised instructional programs and related learning resources through the efforts of state and provincial educational agencies. It distributes productions of individual ETV stations and networks, and sponsors development and production of major consortium projects.

AIT's annually revised catalog describes both types of programs. A subject index, which includes a grade-level key, provides easy access. Program descriptions are arranged alphabetically. Production dates and the number of programs in each series and their running times and titles are clearly set out. In most cases there are also brief to quite full contents summaries. The catalog highlights new releases.

Programs listed in the AIT catalog encompass the entire curriculum and will be recognized as those frequently broadcast on local educational television channels. Videocassettes may be purchased individually and in some states are available through state education departments. A financially attractive way of purchasing individual cassettes rather than the entire series is offered through VideoKits (which consist of up to eight cassettes containing up to thirty-two programs). Having the cassette in the media center means it can be shown when it fits into the instructional design, a method preferable to fitting lessons around a television broadcast. The component titles of each VideoKit are described and contents may be checked by referring back to the main body of the catalog.

VideoKits make available programs such as *If You Go to the Hospital* (from the series *All About You*); *Decisions, Decisions* (from the series *Bread and Butterflies*), a values clarification dramatization involving social ostracism among children; *Energy and Energy Changes* (from the series *Discovering*); *Which Way?* (primary mapping skills from the series *Two Cents Worth*); *Buy and Buy* (consumer education from the series *Inside/Out*); *Buy, Buy, Buy* (primary economics from the series *Two Cents Worth*); *How Will I Grow?* (sex role identification from the series *Ripples*). Individual programs from separate series have also been compiled into VideoKits on *Early Childhood* and *Primary Economics*. Separate programs generally are not over twenty minutes long so that they can be followed by related activities during the same class period.

Sample pages of the AIT Catalog are reproduced on pages 56 through 62. (Reprinted by permission of Agency for Instructional Television.)

1981 AIT CATALOG
of Educational Materials

Elementary
Secondary
In-Service

Broadcast videotape
Videocassette
16 mm film

agency for instructional television

agency for instructional television
box a. bloomington. indiana 47402

1981 AIT Catalog of Educational Materials

Contents

ISSN 0193-5801

Grade Index

JUNIOR HIGH (7-9)

HIGH SCHOOL

Grade Index

The Inside Story with Slim Goodbody

Eight 15-minute color programs
Primary, intermediate
Teacher's guide

Produced for the Wisconsin Television Network by the University of Wisconsin-Green Bay Telecommunications Center, with partial funding from AIT (1981).

Television broadcast fees: see page 115

Audiovisual purchase price:
  Videocassette—$110 per program
  Film—unavailable

  VideoKit—$400
  (See page 122 for more VideoKit information.)

Slim Goodbody, known to many graduates of "Captain Kangaroo," dons his human-body body suit to lead students in grades three through five on a tour of the incredible human body.

Slim (otherwise known as John Burstein) sings and dances his way through huge working models of the human heart, lungs, and digestive system to help children understand what really happens inside their bodies.

He describes the body as a human factory with all parts working in harmony, so that "the most remarkable thing is you." Children learn some basics of health education as Slim explains the good things they must do for the body that works so hard for them.

Interspersed with Slim's explorations are special visuals, good looks at animals whose bodies function differently from ours, and close-up views of our own organs at work, such as a real human heart beating.

PROGRAMS*

1. **Lubba Dubba: The Story of the Human Heart**—Circulation.
2. **The Breath of Life**—Respiration.
3. **Down, Down, Down**—Digestion.
4. **Your Bones and Muscles: The Team That Hustles**—Muscular and skeletal system.
5. **Your Brain and Nervous System: The Smart Part**—Nervous system.
6. **Your Whole Body: The Human Symphony**—Body systems working together.

Two additional programs, for which titles have not yet been determined, will be available in 1981-2. They will cover the senses and the glands.

*Times for programs were unavailable at the time of publication.

BOOKLIST

Chicago: American Library Association, 1905- . Semimonthly (one issue in August). $32.00/yr. (Publisher's address: American Library Association, 50 East Huron Street, Chicago, IL 60611.)

This semimonthly journal reviews primarily books and is addressed primarily to small and medium-sized public libraries. Its "nonprint" coverage is secondary and heavy on films. Filmstrip reviews total between 200 and 250 sets per year, those of video and spoken audio recordings between 100 and 150, and those of slides less than 100. Video programs evaluated here are typically from educational and public television and from independent producers.

One of three general reviewing organs for audiovisuals (the others are *School Library Journal*, page 110, and *Science Books and Films*, page 114), *Booklist* is almost universally subscribed to by libraries, and thus readily available.

Booklist only reviews recent releases and only includes titles it can recommend. Its reviews by staff members and outside reviewers are initialed and critical, indicating intended or appropriate grade levels and supplying Dewey classification numbers and Library of Congress subject headings. They are arranged by medium (only films and filmstrip reviews appear in each issue; other formats are covered at less frequent intervals). Guidelines for reviewers were last printed in the September 1 issue of 1980 and emphasized quality, authenticity, utilization, and techniques relevant for specific formats.

A title index appears in each issue, and these are cumulated semiannually in February and July. The bulk of the entries in these indexes will, of course, be for books.

Booklist reviews are of most help in selecting for social studies and for literature and language arts. Reviews of science and mathematics titles are few. Brief annual lists of "Notable children's filmstrips," compiled by an ALA committee, generally focus on literary titles.

The columns of *Booklist* frequently carry announcements of new professional publications, among them resource guides and mediagraphies on a variety of subjects. It pays to be on the lookout for those announcements.

Sample pages of *Booklist* are reproduced on pages 64 through 66. (Reprinted by permission of the American Library Association from *Booklist*, July 15, 1979, pp. 1640-41, and February 1, 1981, p. 729, copyright © by the American Library Association.)

2/1 booklist

american library association
february 1, 1981
volume 77   number 11
editor
Paul Holm Brawley
books for adults
Bill Ott, editor
Alan Moores, assistant editor
John Brosnahan, reviewer
Denise P. Donavin, reviewer
Julia M. Ehresmann, reviewer
William Bradley Hooper, reviewer
books for young adults
Barbara J. Duree, editor
Sally Estes, reviewer
Stephanie Zvirin, reviewer
children's books
Betsy Hearne, editor
Barbara Elleman, reviewer
Denise M. Wilms, reviewer
nonprint materials
Irene Wood, editor
Beth Ames Herbert, reviewer
Ellen Mandel, reviewer
production manager
Eileen Mahoney
cataloger
Regina Fleischer
indexer
Chere Elliott

booklist editorial advisory board

booklist editorial policy

Booklist is a program of the American Library Association's Publishing Committee. The purpose of *Booklist* is to provide a current guide to materials worthy of consideration for purchase by small and medium-sized public libraries, school media centers, and community college libraries. Materials considered for review, with the exception of books in the non-English-language bibliographies, are limited to works published in English and distributed in the U.S. Textbooks may be evaluated and selected when relevant for library use. Materials which are highly technical, sectarian, or parochial in character, free materials, periodicals, and pamphlets are outside the scope of the regular reviewing program. Standard selection criteria consonant with the Library Bill of Rights and its various interpretations as adopted by the Council of the American Library Association are followed by the *Booklist* staff.

A review in *Booklist* constitutes a recommendation for library purchase. ★ beside a title is a mark of quality, not necessarily of wide appeal or usefulness, and indicates an item selected by the staff as particularly good in its genre. **YA** at the end of an imprint denotes a book also recommended in the Books for Young Adults section. Addresses are given only for publishers and nonprint distributors not listed in the current editions of *Literary Market Place* and *Audiovisual Market Place*.

The *Booklist* editorial and reviewing staff has the responsibility for selection and review of books and nonprint materials in the regular sections. Editors also assign materials to carefully selected field librarians and media and subject specialists. Selection and annotation of items in special lists are the responsibility of the reviewer.

As a general policy *Booklist* does not consider for review books received after publication date: the limit for nonprint materials is three months following release date. *Booklist* uses the Dewey Decimal Classification and Library of Congress subject headings from Cataloging in Publication [CIP] or from the cataloging data of OCLC, Inc. [OCLC]. When these are not available, classification and subject headings assigned by the *Booklist* cataloger are indicated by †.

subscriptions

Booklist is published twice monthly, September through July, and once in August by the American Library Association, 50 East Huron Street, Chicago, Illinois 60611. Subscriptions: USA, Canada, and PUAS countries, $32 per year; other countries $35. Single copy $1.75. Address new subscriptions, renewals, and related correspondence to Robert Nelson, Manager, Membership, Subscription and Order Services. Second-class postage paid at Chicago, Illinois, and at additional mailing offices. (ISSN 0006-7385)

filmstrips

Adjectives and adverbs:
(Grammar for people who hate grammar) Producer: Thompson & Ketchum. Guidance Associates, Communications Park, Box 300, White Plains, NY 10602. 1978. 2 filmstrips (part 1: 58fr., 15min.; part 2: 62fr., 14min.), 2 cassettes, 2 phonodiscs, 10 worksheets, 1 guide, $69.50. #7122.
†425 English language—Adjective || English language—Adverb   78-730153

Nouns.
(Grammar for people who hate grammar) Producer: Thompson & Ketchum. Guidance Associates, Communications Park, Box 300, White Plains, NY 10602. 1978. 2 filmstrips (part 1: 78fr., 15min.; part 2: 64fr., 13min.), 2 cassettes, 2 phonodiscs, 13 worksheets, 1 guide, $69.50. #7171.
†425 English language—Noun   78-730154

Punctuation.
(Grammar for people who hate grammar) Producer: Thompson & Ketchum. Guidance Associates, Communications Park, Box 300, White Plains, NY 10602. 1978. 2 filmstrips (part 1: 106fr., 17min.; part 2: 100fr., 16min.), 2 cassettes, 2 phonodiscs, 14 worksheets, 1 guide, $69.50. #7169.
†425 English language—Punctuation   78-730155

Verbs.
(Grammar for people who hate grammar) Producer: Thompson & Ketchum. Guidance Associates, Communications Park, Box 300, White Plains, NY 10602. 1978. 2 filmstrips (part 1: 59fr., 14min.; part 2: 58fr., 12min.), 2 cassettes, 2 phonodiscs, 14 worksheets, 1 guide, $69.50. #7170.
†425 English language—Verb   78-730156

While *Adjectives and Adverbs* and *Punctuation* structure their presentations around skeletal storylines, *Nouns* and *Verbs* rely on their array of simple cartoons, photos, and vivid graphics to attract viewers to the study of the forms and functions of the parts of speech. Particularly clever visual composition is the highlight of all four sets that imaginatively define the rules and present examples of their applications. Although the filmstrips are quite long, they are organized thoughtfully to facilitate a teacher's showing of one segment at a time. The instructor can then select reinforcing exercises from the guides' suggested activities and from the included worksheets before directing the class on to the succeeding lessons. Prescreening is advised, particularly with *Punctuation,* as teachers may not subscribe to the same rules as the set's producers, but even so these programs will prove helpful for introducing and/or reviewing their topics in middle and junior high school language arts classes. Gr. 5–8. EM.

Basic concepts in psychology.
Producer: Schloat Productions. Prentice-Hall Media, 150 White Plains Rd., Tarrytown, NY 10591. 1979. 4 filmstrips, 4 cassettes, 1 guide, $99. #NYC673. With 4 phonodiscs, $99. #NYR673.
• The psychoanalytic viewpoint. 83fr., 14:40min.
• The behaviorist viewpoint. 95fr., 14:57min.
• The cognitive viewpoint. 82fr., 13:40min.
• The humanistic viewpoint. 77fr., 14:13min.

The contributions of four branches of psychology and their key scholars are clearly summarized in this introductory set through an instructive narration. Graphics, photos, bold silhouettes against striking colors, and special effect photography visually interpret what is basically a non-visual topic; a dilemma that sometimes results in repetitive or contrived frames. This flaw, however, does not seriously detract from the cogent overview of the theories of such psychologists as Freud, Pavlov, Watson, Skinner, Kohler, Piaget, Maslow, and Rogers. Not only are their ideas examined but general criticisms of them by other psychologists are offered. Revealing how these approaches to psychology have influenced the field in general as well as other areas of contemporary life, this presentation will be a beneficial prelude to detailed studies of humanistic, behavioristic, cognitive, and psychoanalytic psychology in high school, community college, and college courses. Viewers interested in another approach to the same topic will wish to compare *Psychology: The Study of Human Behavior,* below. Gr. 9–14. BAH.

†150.19   Psychology—History   78-731068

Basic topics in physical science.
Educational Dimensions Group, Box 126, Stamford, CT 06904. 1978. 4 filmstrips (each approx. 40fr., 10min.) 4 cassettes, 1 guide, $80. #546.
• Matter and atoms.
• Work and energy.
• Electrical energy.
• Light.

Simple definitions and plentiful examples elucidate key concepts and terms involved in the study of physical science. After the first strip describes the properties and states of matter as well as the general process of chemical reactions, the second introduces the formula for work using foot pounds and the law of conservation of matter and energy. In addition to

CHILDREN'S BOOK AND MUSIC CENTER

2500 Santa Monica Boulevard
Santa Monica, CA 90404

The compilers of this mail-order catalog claim it lists "materials which we feel are the best available for all areas of the curriculum." Though selection standards (other than literary and musical quality) are not stated, the conscious effort at pre-selection makes this catalog well worth consulting for preschool and primary materials.

Read-along books, recordings, puzzles, games, pictures, and some filmstrips are offered, along with books for children, teachers, and parents. A very clear subject arrangement groups together materials on basic skills (reading, math, and science), early childhood education, multicultural education, physical education and movement, special education, music, and "emotional and social growth." The latter rubric encompasses a wide range—family relationships, sex education, holidays, community helpers, birth and death, health and safety, feelings, and self-concept. Cross-references alert the user to related materials in other sections, and there is a subject index on the last page. "Multi-Media" (i.e., filmstrips) are grouped together at the beginning of some chapters and interspersed with other formats in others.

The main drawback of this catalog is the fact that it provides no publication or release dates and very little other data, other than two- or three-line contents notes. This presents no problem in the case of recordings of well-known children's books or a $10 kit, but the prospective purchaser of a $100 filmstrip set is entitled to know a bit more before spending such a large sum. Previewing is not available except at a retail showroom in southern California. When contemplating purchasing one of the more expensive items in this catalog, the prudent buyer will want to turn to other sources for further data: To the indicated NICEM Index to learn producer, release date, and extent of visuals (for filmstrips); to *Media Review Digest* for some indication of how the title fared with reviewers; to the producers' catalogs for reproductions of sample visuals and additional data on content and methodology. Part of a set may occasionally be ordered and sampled.

To use this catalog as a lead to what to preview from other sources is not quite the use intended by the distributor. The vast majority of items, however, are modestly priced and can be purchased directly.

Sample pages of the Children's Book and Music Center are reproduced on pages 68 through 70. (Reprinted by permission of the Children's Book & Music Center.)

Contents

CHILDREN'S BOOK AND MUSIC CENTER is a unique single source of phonograph records, books, multi-media, rhythm instruments, and enrichment materials for use by children, teachers and parents.

In this catalog you will find materials which we feel are the best available for all areas of the curriculum, for schools, daycare and parents. Here we have listed outstanding works of music and literature created by artists dedicated to the growth and pleasure of their readers and listeners.

All of the books, recordings, multi-media and instruments in the catalog are on display in our new showroom where you may preview and purchase them. If you prefer, you may order by mail, using the order form in the back, or by phone.

CHILDREN'S BOOK AND MUSIC CENTER is staffed by trained professionals who will help you make suitable and satisfying choices, and will fill your mail orders quickly and efficiently.

ORDERING INFORMATION

■ Use our Order Blank in the back of the catalog—or phone (213-829-0215)

■ We accept Master Charge and Visa Minimum $15.00

■ We bill public schools and agencies—Minimum billing $25.00 Please prepay on orders under $25.00

■ Order by Catalog Number and Title

■ Prices subject to change without notice

■ Minimum postage on Records and Books $2.50 Rhythm Instruments & Audio Equipment extra

■ For Shipping & Handling Charges, see inside back cover

WHEN IN THE LOS ANGELES AREA, VISIT OUR NEW SHOWROOM. LISTEN TO THE RECORDS — SEE THE BOOKS

Our staff will help you choose the proper materials for your specific needs.

CHILDREN'S BOOK AND MUSIC CENTER
2500 Santa Monica Blvd.
Santa Monica, CA. 90404
(213) 829-0215

HOURS:
Monday through Saturday
9 A.M. to 5:30 P.M.
Open Every Sunday in December Before Christmas
11 A.M. to 4 P.M.

Basic Skills In Reading, Math, & Science
Concepts For Early Childhood

LISTEN, SING AND LEARN
A conceptual, motivational program set to music. Simple lyrics and bright melodies entertainingly present primary subjects. By Selma Brody, with narrator-singer Ray Heatherton.

ALL ABOUT DAYS, MONTHS AND SEASONS
If we didn't know what day it was we wouldn't know what to do! 18 songs.

SK134	*Record*	6.95
SK135	*Cassette*	7.95

ALL ABOUT TIME
15 timely" songs.

SK136	*Record*	6.95
SK137	*Cassette*	7.95

ALL ABOUT NUMBERS AND COUNTING
Count instruments of the orchestra, go up in an elevator, counting the floors, count rabbits, etc.

SK138	*Record*	6.95
SK139	*Cassette*	7.95

ALL ABOUT HABITS AND MANNERS
25 songs prepare a child to step into the community.

SK140	*Record*	6.95
SK141	*Cassette*	7.95

ALL ABOUT THE ALPHABET
Traces its history, from grunts to the spoken word - from signals to the written word.

SK142	*Record*	6.95
SK143	*Cassette*	7.95

ALL ABOUT MONEY
Barter and international finance, earning and spending.

SK144	*Record*	6.95
SK145	*Cassette*	7.95

SK146	*Set - 6 Records*	41.70
SK147	*Set - 6 Cassettes*	47.70

MEET MR. MIX-UP
This humorous approach to effective listening and comprehension helps children increase their total listening skills, reading readiness and oral communication. Includes teacher's guide and picture cards.

SK148	*Record*	7.95
SK149	*Cassette*	8.95

MIX AND MATCH ★ EC
Activities for building classification skills with emphasis on applying them to everyday living. Based on a developmental approach to learning, a wide variety of ideas is introduced through a series of progressive levels. Program includes objectives, diagnostic and evaluative tools, pupil worksheets (31 duplicating masters) and games.

SK150	*7" Record w/book*	10.98
SK151	*Book, paper*	8.98

MOTHER GOOSE
69 stories in all, with music and effects by Hershy Kay. Read by Cyril Ritchard, Celeste Holm and Boris Karloff. A very special collection.

SK152	*Record*	6.98
SK153	*Cassette*	7.95

MUSICAL MATH FUN AND GAMES
Through responsive action songs, rhythm methods and activity games, children can understand addition and subtraction better. By Lou Stallman.

SK154	*Record*	6.95

NOISY AND QUIET/BIG AND LITTLE
Musical fun about sounds and sizes told and sung by Tom Glazer, 16 lyric brochures included.

SK155	*Record*	6.98
SK156	*Set - 16 additional lyric brochures*	3.00

OTHER WAY WORDS ★
Songs to teach word opposites, by Willy Strickland and James Earle. A supplementary word growth program for Early Childhood, Special Education, and English As A Second Language. Can be used as teacher-directed with the whole class, in small groups, or independently by children. Music, song, art and humor geared to language development and vocabulary. Contains teacher's guide, pre and post tests, lyrics, preprinted masters for duplicating selected opposite concepts.

SK785	*Two Records*	12.95

RAINDROPS
Rainy day songs and stories, including Eenseyweensey Spider and Three Little Fishes.

SK157	*Record*	5.95

READY-SET-READ-ALONG

A reading readiness program for K-1. Child reads along as letters, numerals, shapes are introduced by games, cartoons, puzzles. Series is self-directing and can be used individually or by entire class. Additional skills gained are concentration, left-right eye movements, visual and auditory discrimination.

DO YOU SEE SILLIES? (BOOK 1)

Introduction to alphabet letters, capital and small.

DO YOU SEE SHAPES? (BOOK 2)

Circle, square, triangle, rectangle in various sizes and positions.

1,2,3 . . . DO YOU SEE NUMBERS & NUMERALS? (BOOK 3)

A visit to a birthday party is the vehicle that introduces numbers and numerals 0-9.

SK158	Set - 3 books w/ 3 records	9.75
SK159	Set - 3 books w/ 3 cassettes	17.75
SK160	Set - 18 books (6 of each) w/ 3 records	25.95
SK161	Set - 18 books (6 of each) w/ 3 cassettes	32.95
SK162	Set - 3 books only	3.50

RHYTHM AND RHYME

An exploration of body movement, hand and finger play. Learning concepts include left and right, up and down, fast and slow, counting and parts of the body.

SK163 *Record*   5.95

SINGING ABOUT COLOR

Jenny Jenkins - Ink is Black - Green-Green-Green - White Coral Bells - Mary Wore Her Red Dress.

SK164 *Record*   6.50

SINGING ABOUT NUMBERS

Honey You Can't Love One - Roll Over - Six Cream Cakes - Sing said the Mother - Clocks - etc.

SK165 *Record*   6.50

SOUND EFFECTS

Street traffic, luncheonette counter, street drilling, department store crowds, etc. Booklet.

SK166 *Record*   6.98

SOUNDS OF NATURE

The 35 sounds include thunder and rain, wind, birds, frogs, night sounds, zoo animals, etc.

SK167 *Record*   6.98

SOUNDS OF THE CITY

The 27 sounds (of Chicago) include jet plane taking off and landing, fireworks, pneumatic drill, cash register, sirens, railroad crossing, etc.

SK168 *Record*   6.98

SOUND-WORD PERCEPTION SKILLS THROUGH MUSIC

Introduces the pre-school child to vowels and consonants through exercises and songs. By Lou Stallman.

SK169 *Record*   6.95

STORIES IN SOUND

Many contrasts of everyday sounds - Loud (Jet Plane, Rocket Blasting Off) - Frightening (Siren) - Funny (Snoring) - Happy (Laughter) - Animal Sounds (Elephant, Monkey, Cow) - Record is not banded.

SK170 *Record*   2.98

TELLING TIME - FACTS & FUN

The history of time telling together with simple explanation of scientific basis for the day, week and year. Album cover is a clock face with movable hands. Teacher's manual.

SK171 *Record*   6.50

More Concepts can be found in following sections - Hap Palmer, Ella Jenkins, Nancy Raven, Marcia Berman and Patty Zeitlin, Bowmar Literature Series and Child's Anthology of Prose and Poetry.

CONCEPTS - Continued next page

CHARLES W. CLARK
168 Express Drive South
Brentwood, NY 11717

A wholesaler of books and audiovisual materials, this company issues an annual free catalog of titles it stocks. With some 5,000 programs from 200 producers listed, this is the most extensive current selection aid. The catalog is arranged in Dewey Decimal order, or as items might be shelved in a library. The page distribution (in the 1980/1981 issue) among the various classes is indicative of subject strengths:

Dewey class	Number of pages
000s	3
100s	13
200s	3
300s	65
400s	7
500s	39
600s	32
700s	27
800s	18
900s	46
Biography	9
Fiction	31
Easy Material	10

Subject access to this catalog is excellent. Its classified arrangement is complemented by a three-page "Quick Reference Index," comprising some 900 keywords, an index from curriculum areas to the Dewey classification (see below), and cross-references within the body of the text. (Some of these are dead ends, however.) There is also a title index. Data supplied for each item listed include, besides order number and price, a brief summary, the intended grade level (coverage is primary through secondary), composition of sets or kits with titles of component parts, and prices of parts that are available separately. Release dates are not uniformly given. In many cases, there are references (with dates) to reviews in professional journals. Without page numbers, these are hard to locate. Producer and catalog card availability are indicated; an asterisk (*) denotes material added during the current year. Material for junior and senior high school grades is also easily spotted with a ●symbol next to it.

The vast majority of the listings are for filmstrips and multimedia kits, but cassettes, records, filmloops, transparencies, and study prints are also represented.

Listing in this catalog should in no way be regarded as a recommendation as would be the case in such selective tools as the *Core Collections* or *The Elementary School Library Collection*. Included titles are merely, one assumes, those that the Clark Company finds the most salable, and the catalog is a convenient spot for an initial look. In most cases, further checking will be required, similar to that required for a title located in any vendor catalog. This may reveal some titles to be ten or more years old.

The company does extend fifteen-day previewing privileges on materials other than single records, cassettes, posters, filmloops, or transparencies.

Sample pages of the Clark catalog are reproduced on pages 72 through 74.

Because this catalog is organized by **Dewey Decimal Classification** no page numbers are given. **Dewey Classification appears on the top corner of each page.**

CURRICULUM AREAS	DEWEY DECIMAL CLASSIFICATION
ARTS & CRAFTS	700-790
BIOGRAPHY	
Collective Biography	920
Explorers	910.92
Individual biography	B (following section 920)
Musicians	780.92
CAREER EDUCATION	331.702
ENGLISH LITERATURE	800-829
Anthologies	808; 808.8
Drama	808.2; 812; 822
Fiction	F (following 999); 808.3
Poetry	808.1; 811; 821
Writing, Composition	808.06
FOLKLORE, FAIRY TALES, FABLES	398.2
FOREIGN LANGUAGES	830-899; 418
French	440; 840
German	430; 830
Italian	450; 850
Spanish	460; 860
GUIDANCE	155-177; 371.4; 331.702
HEALTH EDUCATION	609-615
Drugs	613.8
Family Life	301.4; 612.6
Safety	614.8
HOME ECONOMICS	640-649
Consumer Education	640.73
LANGUAGE ARTS	372.6; 420-429; E; F; 398.2
Children's Stories	F (following 999); E (following F)
Composition	808.06; 428
Grammar	425
Reading	372.4
Spelling	421.5
LIBRARY SKILLS	020-029
MATHEMATICS	510-516
Metrics	389
MUSIC	780-789
PHYSICAL EDUCATION	613.7
Sports	796-799
READING	372.4
SAFETY	614.8
SCIENCE	520-599
Chemistry	540-549
Earth Sciences	550-599
Life Sciences (Biology)	570-599
Physics	530-539
Technology	620-630
SOCIAL STUDIES	300-369; 900-999
Economics	330-339
Geography	900-919
Government	320-329
History	930-999
SPECIAL EDUCATION	371.9
VOCATIONAL EDUCATION	610; 620-629; 650-699

Audio Visual Materials

536 HEAT

The following sets also contain material related to heat:
Energy and man - VP3 (531.6)
Investigating relationships in matter - MY5 (500)
Taking a good look at science - TR3 (530)
Weather and climate - TR3 (551.5)
Whys of elementary science - FH3 (500)

536 Film Loop		P-I

ELEMENTARY SCIENCE: Heat Super-8mm film loops, 4 min. each. 1971

UN6-6623	How heat affects metal	
UN6-6645	Heat conduction in solids	
UN6-6646	Kindling	
UN6-6730	Making a simple thermometer	
UN6-6732	Heat convection in water	
UN6-6771	Sources of heat	
UN6-6772	Heat transfer by radiation	
UN6-6773	Color affects radiant heat	
UN6-6774	Is paper an insulator?	
UN6-6775	Most solids melt	
Each FL; Ge		**22.00**

536 Filmstrip-Sound		I

HEAT This program explains the concept of heat as a form of energy, deals with molecular motion, illustrates the nature of burning and oxidation, discusses all sources of heat and how it is transferred. 1970

EA5-407	Set of 2-FS; 1-CA; Ge	22.00

536 Transparency		I-J

HEAT An introduction to key concepts.

DC7-27	Set of 10-TR	35.95

536 Film Loop		P-I

HEAT AND TEMPERATURE These film loops have short label-captions so students can follow along with ease. Each 4 min. 1973

TR6-5116	What is temperature?	
TR6-5117	How a thermometer works	
TR6-5118	What does heat do?	
TR6-5119	How does heat travel?	
TR6-5120	**Set of 4-FL**	**99.80**
Each FL		**24.95**

537 ELECTRICITY , ELECTRONICS

The following sets also contain material related to electricity and electronics:
Basic physical science - IF5 (500.2)
How things work and why - TR6 (500.2)
Jackdaws - VI8 (659.13)
Science adventures - FH3 (500)
Science fundamentals - UN3 (500)
Science in your world: Intermediate - MI4 (500)
Taking a good look at science - TR3 (530)
Whys of elementary science - FH3 (500)
Wonders of science - TR3 (530)

537 Print		I-J

ELECTRICITY Diagrammatic science study prints. 1971

MI8-1652	Set of 8-PR; 4-DM; Ge	8.95

537 Transp. Dupl. Book		I-J

ELECTRICITY Milliken transparency duplicating book. 1969

MI7-1305	TDB of 12-TR; 4-DM; Ge	6.95

537 Transparency		I-J

ELECTRICITY An introduction to key concepts.

DC7-22	Magnetism (5-TR; 6-VIS)	21.95
DC7-23	Static electricity (6-TR; 7-VIS)	
		27.95
DC7-24	Current electricity (10-TR; 17-VIS)	
		44.95
DC7-25	**Complete set of 21-TR; 30-VIS**	**89.00**

537 Film Loop		I-J-H

● **ELECTRICITY: Cells and circuits**

ES6-9368	The circuit	
ES6-9369	The galvanometer	
ES6-9370	Liquid conductors, Part 1	
ES6-9371	Liquid conductors, Part 2	
ES6-9372	The wet cell	
ES6-9373	Parallel circuits	
ES6-9374	Series circuits	
ES6-9367	**Set of 7-FL; Ge**	**175.00**
Each FL		**26.95**

537 Transparency		J-H-C

● **ELECTRICITY/BASIC ELECTRONICS** This series illustrates important electrical laws, beginning with simple electrical theory and progressing to transistors and radar. Ask for DCA catalog. 1971

DC7-76	Electrostatics (13-TR; 30-VIS)	
		79.50
DC7-77	Voltage sources (7-TR; 12-VIS)	
		36.00
DC7-78	Fundamental electrical principles (5-TR; 12-VIS)	35.50
DC7-79	Electrolysis (3-TR; 7-VIS)	22.50
DC7-80	Magnetism & electromagnetism (15-TR; 21-VIS)	87.50
DC7-81	Machines (8-TR; 10-VIS)	39.50
DC7-82	Inductance (3-TR; 5-VIS)	17.75
DC7-83	Meters (3-TR; 4-VIS)	15.50
DC7-84	Alternating current (19-TR; 40-VIS)	
		112.50
DC7-85	Vacuum tube fundamentals (9-TR; 16-VIS)	37.50
DC7-2	Semi-conductors & transistors (7-TR; 8-VIS)	36.50
DC7-3	Special purpose tubes (3-TR; 3-VIS)	15.25
DC7-4	Antennas/Electronic systems (2-TR; 3-VIS)	14.75
DC7-75	**Complete set: 104-TR; 179-VIS**	**600.00**

537   Film Loop   **J-H**

● **ELECTRICITY — ELECTRONICS SERIES** This
34 film series is an introduction to the fascinating
world of electricity and electronics. 1973

PH6-724   Electricity produced by friction
PH6-725   Electricity produced by pressure,
heat and light
PH6-726   Electricity produced by chemical action-I
PH6-727   Electricity produced by chemical action - II
PH6-728   Electricity produced by magnetism - I
PH6-729   Electricity produced by magnetism - II
PH6-730   Electromagnetism
PH6-731   Conductors and insulators
PH6-732   Current flow and measurement
PH6-733   Voltage and voltage measurement
PH6-734   Resistance
PH6-735   Resistance measurement & color
code
PH6-736   Series circuits - I (Current)
PH6-737   Series circuits - II (Voltage)
PH6-738   Series circuits - III (Resistance)
PH6-739   Parallel circuits - I (Current)
PH6-740   Parallel circuits - II (Voltage)
PH6-741   Parallel circuits - III (Resistance)
PH6-742   Ohm's Law theory - I
PH6-743   Ohm's Law theory - II
PH6-744   Ohm's Law formula $I = E/R$
PH6-745   Ohm's Law formula $E = I \times R$
PH6-746   Ohm's Law formula $R = E/I$
PH6-747   The diodes
PH6-748   The half-wave rectifier - I   (Using
vacuum tube)
PH6-749   The half-wave rectifier - II   (Using
semiconductor)
PH6-750   The full-wave rectifier - I   (Using
vacuum tube)
PH6-751   The full-wave rectifier - II (Using semi-
conductor)
PH6-752   The bridge rectifier
PH6-753   Filter circuits - I
PH6-754   Filter circuits - II
PH6-755   The complete power supply - I (Half-
wave vacuum tube rectifier; filter)
PH6-756   The complete power supply - II (Full-
wave vacuum tube rectifier; filter)

PH6-757   The complete power supply - III
(Bridge rectifier; using semiconductor diodes;
L filter)
Each FL   **26.00**
Consult Thorne catalog for full information.

537   Transparency   **J-H-V**

● **ELECTRICITY ONE-SEVEN** A complete training
program in 2-color visual presentations treating
the fundamentals of electricity. The individual
sets are arranged in convenient sub-sets so that
the instructor can easily custom fit them to any
existing or planned course schedule. The visuals
are uncluttered for easy adaptation and hand
marking by the instructor. 1967

UT7-7381   Electricity and magnetism, Set I
(53-TR)   **114.00**
UT7-7441   Direct-current circuits, Set II (74-
TR)   **159.00**
UT7-7525   Alternating-current circuits, Set III
(102-TR)   **219.00**

UT7-7637   LCR and resonant circuits, Set IV
(108-TR)   **232.00**
UT7-7759   Test equipment, Set V (67-TR)
144.00
UT7-7832   Batteries, Set VI (41-TR)   **88.00**
UT7-7880   Generators, Set VII (63-TR)
136.00
UT7-7946   Motors, Set VIII (105-TR)
225.00
UT7-7380   Complete series: 613-TR   1250.00
Consult United Transparencies catalog for
additional information.

537   Transparency   **J-H-V**

● **ELECTRONICS ONE-SEVEN** This series presents information vital to an understanding of the
principles of electronics and electronic devices. A
second color is used to emphasize important
points and features. The individual sets are arranged in sub-sets so that the instructor can easily
custom fit them to any existing or planned course
schedule:

UT7-2001   Signals, Set I (83-TR)   **178.45**
UT7-2092   Electronic building blocks, Set II
(76-TR)   **163.40**
UT7-2179   The electron tube, Set III (74-TR)
159.10
UT7-2260   Semiconductors, Set IV (87-TR)
187.05
UT7-2358   Circuits, Set V (246-TR)   **528.90**
UT7-2627   Antennas, Set VI (56-TR)   **120.00**
UT7-2000   Complete set of 622-TR   1270.45
Consult United Transparencies catalog for
additional information.

537   Film Loop   **P-I**

ELEMENTARY SCIENCE: Electric circuit Su-
per-8mm film loops, each about 4 min. 1971

UN6-6071   The electric circuit
UN6-6072   Dry cells in series
UN6-6073   Examining your flashlight
UN6-6074   The electrical switch
UN6-6075   Electrical conductors
UN6-6076   Incandescent lamp
UN6-6077   Making a dry cell
UN6-6078   Lamps in series
UN6-6079   How the flashlight works
UN6-6080   The fuse
UN6-6070   Set of 10-FL; Ge   220.00
Each FL; Ge   22.00

537   Film Loop   **I-J-H**

● **FRICTION TRANSFERS ELECTRONS** Seven
film loops show the behavior of electrons if sub-
jected to friction. Concept deals with positive and
negative charges as well as electrostatic induction. 1972

ES6-9360   Positive charge
ES6-9361   Negative charge
ES6-9362   Polarity of static charges
ES6-9363   Insulators and conductors
ES6-9364   Electrostatic induction
ES6-9365   Electroscope, Part 1
ES6-9366   Electroscope, Part 2
ES6-9359   Set of 6-FL; Ge   175.00
Each FL   26.95

CORE MEDIA COLLECTION FOR ELEMENTARY SCHOOLS

Lucy Gregor Brown. New York: Bowker, 1978. 224p. $17.50.
(Publisher's address: R. R. Bowker, 1180 Avenue of the
Americas, New York, NY 10036.)

Approximately 1,400 recommended titles released in the main between 1973
and 1977 are found here, including a few 16mm films in addition to filmstrips, slides,
filmloops, and recordings. The *Core Collection* represents a compilation of recommendations by many sources, from the American Association for the Advancement
of Science to the *Wilson Library Bulletin*, and including professional publications in
many disciplines. Those sources are indicated (with dates) in each entry, which also
supplies running times, number of frames for filmstrips, release dates, grade levels,
titles of component parts, and fairly full summaries. All areas of the curriculum are
covered.

Core Media Collection for Elementary Schools is intended by its publisher as an
update to *Resources for Learning* (1971). One hopes that less than a seven-year
interval between editions will be observed in the future. Even were the interval
reduced to the four years between editions of its companion titles, *Core Media Collection for Secondary Schools*, this work would still remain second choice to the
Elementary School Library Collection with its more frequent revision schedule. There
is some overlap between the two works. *Elementary School Library Collection*,
however, contains more titles and is notably more lavish in its coverage of recordings.

Since *Core Media Collection for Elementary Schools* is by the same author and
quite similar to *Core Media Collection for Secondary Schools*, what is said there
(pp. 77-78) about subject searching applies here as well.

The title page of the *Core Media Collection for Elementary Schools* is reproduced on page 76. (Reprinted by permission of R. R. Bowker Company. Copyright
© 1978 by Xerox Corporation.)

CORE MEDIA COLLECTION FOR ELEMENTARY SCHOOLS

Lucy Gregor Brown

Assisted by

Betty McDavid,
Technical Librarian,
Mt. Diablo Unified School District

R. R. Bowker Company
New York & London, 1978

CORE MEDIA COLLECTION FOR SECONDARY SCHOOLS

Lucy Gregor Brown. 2nd ed. New York: Bowker, 1979.
263p. $18.95. (Publisher's address: R. R. Bowker, 1180
Avenue of the Americas, New York, NY 10036.)

This useful tool, published in late 1979, recommends approximately 1,500 filmstrip sets and other media titles released through 1978 that "have been favorably reviewed, are award winners, or have been evaluated for their authenticity, technical quality, student level, interest and motivation, accuracy in contents, and validity in treatment" (p. vii). Though some of the items noted are by now ten years old, this is still the first place to look for secondary media. It supplements the first edition (1975) that performed a similar service for media released from the 1960s through 1973. All types of audiovisual media, including films, and all curriculum areas are included.

Arrangement of this catalog is alphabetical by subject, using the *Sears List of Subject Headings* supplemented with idiosyncratic headings. Cross-references are supplied. The user would do well to look both to the more general topic and to related topics. For example, looking for titles on "Newspapers" turns up *What Is Journalism?* and a reference to "Journalism" for more complete information. Two other titles of possible relevance (*Free Press* and *Satirical Journalism*) are found by turning to that listing. Pursuing possible related terms, there are additional entries under "Mass Media" (*This Business Called Media*) and "Propaganda" (*What's Going On Here?*).

Following up every possible related reference works equally well when proceeding from the general to the specific, as in the case of "Home Economics," which leads to "Interior Decoration," "Clothing and Dress," "Consumer Education," "Nutrition," "Houses," "Hygiene," and "Lifestyles—U.S.," and from there to "Sewing," "Advertising," "Credit," "Shopping," "Cookery," and more.

The title index should not be overlooked when conducting a subject search: the filmstrip *Energy* is not found under either "Force and Energy" or "Power Resources." Only the titles of sets, not those of individual filmstrips, are noted in the indexes.

Data supplied in each entry are as noted for the companion volume, the *Core Media Collection for Elementary Schools* (see pages 75-76).

The title page of the *Core Media Collection for Secondary Schools* is reproduced on page 78. (Reprinted with permission of R. R. Bowker Company. Copyright © 1979 by Xerox Corporation.)

CORE MEDIA COLLECTION FOR SECONDARY SCHOOLS

Second Edition

Lucy Gregor Brown

Assisted by

Betty McDavid,
Technical Librarian,
Mt. Diablo Unified School District

R. R. Bowker Company
New York & London, 1979

THE ELEMENTARY SCHOOL LIBRARY COLLECTION

Lois Winkel, ed. 13th ed. Newark, NJ: Bro-Dart, 1982. 1104p. $39.95. (Publisher's address: Bro-Dart Foundation, 1807 Pembroke Road, Greensboro, NC 27408.)

In selecting for elementary schools, the *Elementary School Library Collection* is the first stop. Published biennially, sometimes with updates in alternate years, it recommends books for both students and teachers, as well as most audiovisual formats except films. It contains more audiovisual titles, is more frequently revised, and provides far more content per dollar than the *Core Collection for Elementary Schools*.

A total of 1,768 audiovisual titles released through 1980 are found in the thirteenth edition, published in early 1982, in addition to over 8,000 books. Arrangement is by Dewey Decimal Classification—handy for shelf-checking and capable of doubling as a catalog. There are over 1,000 sound filmstrip sets. The remainder are filmloops, games, slides, captioned filmstrip sets, transparency sets, and charts.

The editors state the criteria for admission to this collection as "quality, appeal to children, excellence in format, authenticity of content" and assert that an "effort has been made to include titles . . . which effectively portray attitudes of mutual respect and understanding among all people." Further, "as a rule, a filmstrip or recording based on a book is not recommended unless the book itself can be recommended." (pp. vii, ix).

Each entry supplies title of set, titles, running times, number of frames of component strips, producer or distributor, release date, order number, price, a brief synopsis, and subject headings.

If the Dewey classification for the wanted subject is known, it is easiest to proceed to that section directly. Checking the Subject Index, however, will generally lead to titles in other portions of the catalog as well. That index employs the *Sears List of Subject Headings* and makes references to class, not page, numbers. Formats, other than book, are clearly indicated. It pays to look under every possible term. A filmstrip about Ellis Island, for instance, is contained in the set *Early American Experience*, but looking only under "Immigration and Emigration" would never locate it. ("Ellis Island" is the only subject heading used.)*

Another hint, once a quite relevant title has been located, is to note the last two lines of the entry (starting with "SUBJ"). These are the subject headings assigned to that item. Following those up may lead one to others equally in point. For example, "Blood Pressure" indexes *Heart and Circulatory System*. Another heading for that set is "Heart—Diseases," which when found in the subject index refers one to *Enemies of the Body*, which turns out to contain a strip on *Hypertension*, i.e., high blood pressure.

The Dewey Decimal arrangement permits browsing, as it does on library shelves. Without it, it might be difficult to find materials on the Pacific Ocean islands for someone who would not think of looking up "Islands of the Pacific" in the index. Trying "New Zealand," one is directed to 919.31. Just above that number, there is *Seeing the Pacific Islands*.

---

*The examples and accompanying illustrations are from the twelfth edition.

The title index is also worth pursuing for possible titles starting with one's keyword.

It is difficult to estimate the subject distribution of the media included in this volume. Many of the recordings are musical recordings; folktales are also heavily represented. Coverage is probably more intensive in social studies than in science.

Sample pages of *The Elementary School Library Collection* are reproduced below and on page 81. (Reprinted by permission of Bro-Dart Elementary School Library Collection.)

THE ELEMENTARY SCHOOL LIBRARY COLLECTION

A GUIDE TO BOOKS AND OTHER MEDIA

TWELFTH EDITION   PHASES 1-2-3

Lois Winkel — Editor

Assisted by
Margaret Edsall
Dorothy Fix
Elizabeth Friggle
Mary Virginia Gaver
Bette Gorton
Kathryn S. Howie
Irene Johnson
Ethel Kutteroff
Robert E. Muller
Lynn Vrooman
Linda Worden
Phyllis Yuill

THE BRO-DART FOUNDATION

Newark, New Jersey

1979

NON-FICTION

612   Ph-1 I-5 $4.99   DF711
HAMMOND, WINIFRED G. Riddle of teeth. Coward-McCann c1971.
60p illus.
   Most chapters of this factual book about teeth contain interesting
   projects for readers to try at home or in school with other classmates.
   The author is very specific in her discussion of the formation of teeth,
   the different kinds of teeth and how they work, the causes of caries
   and other dental diseases, and the fight to control and prevent the
   loss of teeth. Children who are preparing for orthodontia can learn
   much from this book, and it can be used in health classes, by dentists,
   and for general reading about the care and protection of the teeth
   and mouth.
   SUBJ: Teeth.

FSS 612   Ph-2 I $49.50   DF712
HEART AND CIRCULATORY SYSTEM (FILMSTRIP) Guidance Associates
7141-1310, 1977. 2 filmstrips color, 1 cassette and 1 phonodisc. (Your
body and how to care for it series)
   Same material is on both cassette and phonodisc.
   Describes the heart and circulatory system, blood composition, blood
   pressure, diseases of the circulatory system, and how to avoid heart
   trouble. With teacher's guide.
   Contents: Pt. 1, 55fr/11min; Pt. 2, 63fr/11min.
   SUBJ: Heart./ Blood--Circulation./ Blood./ Blood pressure./ Heart--
   Diseases.

612   Ph-3 A-10 $4.00   DF713
HEINTZE, CARL. Priceless pump, the human heart. Nelson; In Canada:
Don Mills, Ontario; Thomas Nelson & Sons (Canada) Ltd. 1972. 128p
illus.
   Includes index.

FSS 616   Ph-2 I-A $64.00   DF850
ENEMIES OF THE BODY (FILMSTRIP) Educational Activities FSC 487,
1976. 4 filmstrips color, 4 cassettes.
   Describes four major diseases, discussing symptoms, physical and
   laboratory findings, physical changes, causes, treatment and
   prevention. With teacher's guides.
   Contents: Cancer--What is it? 54fr/13min; Hypertension--The quiet
   killer, 49fr/12min; The heart attack--Sudden terror, 52fr/13min;
   Diabetes--Sugar gone awry, 51fr/11min.
   SUBJ: Diseases./ Cancer./ Hypertension./ Heart--Diseases./ Diabetes.

KIT 616.01   Ph-2 A $5.95   DF851
CRELLIN, J. K., COMP. Pasteur and the germ theory (Kit) Jackdaw; dist.
by Viking 1968. items. (Jackdaw, no. 53)
   A heavy-duty envelope containing contemporary documents, portraits,
   diagrams and charts explaining Pasteur's discovery. Contents folder
   contains annotated Notes on the exhibits, and suggestions to Think
   for yourself and Do it yourself. Especially useful is Chart showing
   various aspects of vaccination.
   SUBJ: Germ theory of disease./ Pasteur, Louis.

GREAT PLAINS NATIONAL INSTRUCTIONAL
TELEVISION LIBRARY
Box 80669
Lincoln, NE 68501

GPN, like AIT (pages 55-62), is a source for instructional television series in video formats. Its catalog, revised annually, is free. The latest issue contains over 100 series, many of them familiar offerings of educational channels. Featured in a separate section are eighteen series "developed to improve understanding among individuals of different ethnic, cultural or racial backgrounds" (among them *Vegetable Soup*). These are eligible for acquisition with Emergency School Aid Act (ESAA) funds.

Grade level and subject indexes are guides to the separate sections which detail programs for elementary and secondary grades. Production dates and the number of programs in a series, including their titles and frequently their content, are described. Most programs are fifteen to twenty minutes in length, with some extending to thirty minutes, and most are accompanied by teachers' materials.

New series are highlighted in the catalog, which also serves as the distribution vehicle for the slide sets compiled by the National Council for Geographic Education. Sixty-one of the programs are primarily for elementary schools, while twenty-six are primarily for junior and senior high schools and up. Distribution among subject areas appears to be fairly even, although the science series are all for the middle school level and below.

Sample pages of the Great Plains National Instructional Television Library catalog are reproduced on pages 83 through 86. (Reprinted by permission of Great Plains National Instructional Television Library.)

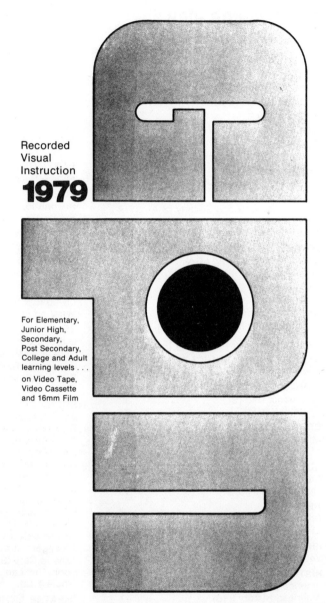

Recorded
Visual
Instruction
1979

For Elementary,
Junior High,
Secondary,
Post Secondary,
College and Adult
learning levels . . .
on Video Tape,
Video Cassette
and 16mm Film

• *Off-Air Recording Policy . . . see* **Inside Front Cover**   • *New Pricing Structure . . . see* **Page 162**

JUNIOR HIGH
SECONDARY
ADULT

Page

UTILIZATION
IN-SERVICE

COLLEGE

What's New for 1981!

NOTE: The new materials described above are identified throughout the catalog by the appearance of large stars, like the one above, on the description pages. It should also be noted that three older GPN series have been expanded with the addition of new programs. They include: EMERGING PLAYWRIGHTS, page 133 (2 new programs); THE NCGE/ GPN SLIDES, page 129 (6 new sets); and ROOMNASTICS, page 30 (8 new programs).

THE GUIDE TO SIMULATIONS/GAMES FOR EDUCATION AND TRAINING

4th edition. Robert E. Horn and Anne Cleaves, eds. Sage Publications, 1980. 692p. $49.95. (Publisher's address: Sage Publications, 275 South Beverly Drive, Beverly Hills, CA 90212.)

Any high school or community college educator who desires to use gaming as a teaching device will need this volume. News and reviews of simulations appear only in specialized journals devoted to gaming and computing, and not many media centers or libraries are likely to subscribe to those.

Over 1,000 games that were on the market in January 1979 and were intended for academic and school settings are noted (there is also a much shorter listing of published business simulations). Separate essays evaluate leading games in different subject areas, including communications, ecology, economics, energy, futures, history, international relations, politics, sex roles, and other topics relevant to social science studies in high school and college.

Several hundred of the games are new to this edition, the previous one having been published in 1977. They are not identified as such in the volume.

The book has 25 chapters dealing with the following topics:

Addictions	Human Services
Communication	International Relations
Community Issues	Language Skills and Art
Computer Simulations	Legal System
Domestic Politics	Mathematics
Ecology	Military History
Economics	Practical Economics
Education	Religion
Frame Games	Science
Futures	Self-Development
Geography	Social Studies
Health	Urban
History	

The absence of a subject index is a serious drawback. Without it, the user must scan an entire chapter to find a desired topic. Copyright dates are prominently displayed in each entry, however, making the identification of recent releases quite easy.

Other notations under "playing data" indicate age level, number of players, playing time, and packaging. Full analytical descriptions, some several paragraphs in length, provide not only content but also critical evaluations for potential applications. Many of these are based on actual classroom usage. If a game is discussed in one of the initial evaluative essays, this is noted and a reference included. Producer's name and address and price (as of January 1979) are supplied, making each entry self-contained and a complete source of needed data for ordering.

To update the *Guide*, place your name on the mailing lists of major producers such as:

Ampersand Press	Bobbs Merrill Co.
Avalon Hill Co.	Carolina Biological Supply Co.
(specialize in war games)	Center for Simulation Studies

Changing Times Education
Service
Conflict Games
Edu-Game
Games Central

History Simulations
Interact
Simile II
Wff'n Poof

Sample pages of *The Guide to Simulations/Games for Education and Training* are reproduced below and on pages 89 through 91. (Reprinted with permission by the publisher, Sage Publications, Beverly Hills.)

The Guide to
Simulations / Games
for education
and training

4th Edition

Robert E. Horn
and
Anne Cleaves

Editors

 **SAGE** PUBLICATIONS   Beverly Hills   London

CONTENTS

LIBRARY JOURNAL

New York: Bowker, 1876- . Semimonthly (monthly in July
and August). $38.00/yr. (Publisher's address: R. R. Bowker,
1180 Avenue of the Americas, New York, NY 10036.)

Library Journal's "Audiovisual Review," appearing in each semimonthly issue,
has the same editor as *School Library Journal's* companion "Audiovisual Review"
section. The reviews themselves are similar in every respect to those appearing in that
journal, except for being aimed at an older age level. Films predominate among the
twenty to twenty-five titles evaluated per month. Many of them and the recordings,
slides, filmstrip sets, and multimedia kits are suitable for high school and early college-
level instruction as well. They concentrate heavily on topics of current interest.
There is no index.

An "Audiovisual Showcase" appeared in the January 1982 issue and listed, from
distributor-supplied data, approximately 400 late 1981 and projected early 1982
releases. The intended audience is stated as being high school through college and
adult. The subject arrangement in approximately sixty categories permits one to
readily survey current production. This and the companion "AV Forecast" in *School
Library Journal* are the only means of obtaining such an overview. Physical description, running times, prices, and other ordering information are supplemented by
brief contents notes.

Sample pages of the *Library Journal* are reproduced on pages 93 and 94.
(Reprinted with permission from *Library Journal* [October 1, 1982, page 1843].
R. R. Bowker Company/A Xerox Corporation. Copyright © 1982 by Xerox
Corporation.)

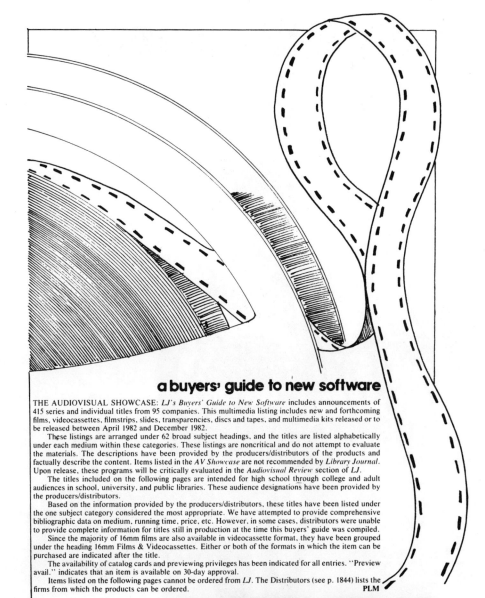

a buyers' guide to new software

THE AUDIOVISUAL SHOWCASE: *LJ's Buyers' Guide to New Software* includes announcements of 415 series and individual titles from 95 companies. This multimedia listing includes new and forthcoming films, videocassettes, filmstrips, slides, transparencies, discs and tapes, and multimedia kits released or to be released between April 1982 and December 1982.

These listings are arranged under 62 broad subject headings, and the titles are listed alphabetically under each medium within these categories. These listings are noncritical and do not attempt to evaluate the materials. The descriptions have been provided by the producers/distributors of the products and factually describe the content. Items listed in the *AV Showcase* are not recommended by *Library Journal*. Upon release, these programs will be critically evaluated in the *Audiovisual Review* section of *LJ*.

The titles included on the following pages are intended for high school through college and adult audiences in school, university, and public libraries. These audience designations have been provided by the producers/distributors.

Based on the information provided by the producers/distributors, these titles have been listed under the one subject category considered the most appropriate. We have attempted to provide comprehensive bibliographic data on medium, running time, price, etc. However, in some cases, distributors were unable to provide complete information for titles still in production at the time this buyers' guide was compiled.

Since the majority of 16mm films are also available in videocassette format, they have been grouped under the heading 16mm Films & Videocassettes. Either or both of the formats in which the item can be purchased are indicated after the title.

The availability of catalog cards and previewing privileges has been indicated for all entries. "Preview avail." indicates that an item is available on 30-day approval.

Items listed on the following pages cannot be ordered from *LJ*. The Distributors (see p. 1844) lists the firms from which the products can be ordered. **PLM**

AUDIOVISUAL
SHOWCASE

JANUARY 1, 1982   (ISSN 0363-0277)

LIBRARY JOURNAL

LJ Award-winning Films and Videotapes of 1981
Videoworks at the Tucson Public Library
New England LA Conference Report

In the News: ACRL symposium heralds technological era;
Pittsburgh conference eyes challenge and change

AV SHOWCASE

MEDIA REVIEW DIGEST

Ann Arbor, MI: Pierian Press, 1981. Annual. 767p. $150.00.
(Publisher's address: Pierian Press, P. O. Box 1808, Ann
Arbor, MI 48106.)

This index to media reviews, published annually, is helpful for retrospective searches. It provides at a glance knowledge of

a) how a known title was received by the critics; and

b) the most favorable reviewed media on a particular topic in
a given year.

Each volume synthesizes the reviews of the previous year, which in turn may have critiqued titles released perhaps a year or more earlier. Lagtime is thus about two years, and the 1981 volume, with reviews published in 1980, covers releases of 1979-1980 and earlier.

Arrangement is by title in four sections, covering Films and Videotapes, Filmstrips, Records and Tapes, and Miscellaneous Media. The latter comprises kits, slides, transparencies, slide/tape sets, etc. If checking a filmstrip title, "Miscellaneous" must be consulted as well since some of the entries are placed there.

Under the entry for each title can be found the name of producer, release date, items included with their length and numbers of visuals (for slides and filmstrip kits), and price (these data are all taken from the review, and prices thus are not current and only an indication of general price range). Dewey Decimal Classification, Library of Congress subject headings (supplemented with some idiosyncratic ones), grade-level indication, and a one-sentence note about contents follow, after which there is a listing, with dates, volume, and page numbers of reviews in one or more periodicals. Each is preceded by a "+" or "–," or in some cases an asterisk (*), indicating the title was only mentioned in the source and not critically reviewed. Excerpts from reviews and names of reviewers are given on occasion.

Reference can be made directly to the title listings for titles tentatively chosen from a vendor catalog or similar source, perhaps one labeled "new." It may be two or three years old and a review noted in a recent volume.

There are three ways to conduct a subject search in *Media Review Digest*. Depending on how broad the topic is, the search may start either with the "alphabetical subject index" or the "General Subject Indicators." in the 1980 volume, the latter shows, e.g., forty-seven titles under "Women," while the Alphabetical Subject Index pinpoints titles of "Women artists," "Women–Employment," etc., and, through cross-references, "Feminists," "Mothers," "Self-defense for Women," and many more. Finally, there is a "Classified Subject Index" that lists all titles in the volume by Dewey Decimal Numbers, as they would be shelved in a library. This serves when a class number is known and one is certain one wants to limit the search to that class number. Note that only twenty-three titles on "Women" are listed under 301.412, or half of those retrieved through the General Subject Index.

Media Review Digest's high price reflects its broad coverage, which extends to entertainment films and many more musical recordings than would interest a school or college media center. Various ancillary features include a listing of mediagraphies, concentrating heavily on individual producers, filmmakers, and actors.

The expense of having an up-to-date set of *Media Review Digest* is not justified for any but the largest media centers, film study collections, or college learning centers, but the media specialist in even the small school would do well to know where a nearby set is located and consult it as the need arises. That will perhaps be only once a year, when preparing the major order. It will also be worth the effort to check this source—going back no more than two years—for subjects flagged by needs assessment. The information retrieved will provide a base from which to start the search through vendor catalogs.

Sample pages of the *Media Review Digest* are reproduced below and on pages 97 through 101. (Reprinted by permission of The Pierian Press, copyright © 1979 by The Pierian Press. All rights reserved.)

MEDIA

REVIEW

DIGEST

1979

THE ONLY COMPLETE GUIDE

TO REVIEWS OF NON-BOOK MEDIA

MRD

FILMS AND VIDEOTAPES
FILMSTRIPS
RECORDS AND TAPES
MISCELLANEOUS MEDIA

edited by Elinor J. Schwartz

THE PIERIAN PRESS
Ann Arbor, Michigan
1979

CONTENTS

ALPHABETICAL SUBJECT INDEX

GENERAL SUBJECT INDICATORS

Helpers: Personalizing the teaching of reading
Implications for teaching (FS)
The language experience approach to teaching reading
Learning resources
Max made mischief: An approach to literature
The OK classroom
The parent crunch
The sooner the better
Teacher training in values education: A workshop (series) (FS)
Teaching beginning reading (MM)
When I grow up . . .
Working in the integrated classroom (MM)
TECHNICAL TRAINING see VOCATIONAL AND TECHNICAL
    TRAINING
TECHNOLOGY AND ENGINEERING
    An Alaskan adventure (MM)
    Aluminum – Magnesium – Metals for our time
    America rock: Mother Necessity
    Armand Hardy, menuisier – tonnelier
    Atomic power production
    Basic construction techniques (series) (FS)
    The beauty of bending
    The breeder
    Bridge to tomorrow
    Brittle and rubbery materials (MM)
    Building audits for energy conservation (series)
    Clear to land
    Composites (MM)
    The computer parts kit (MM)
    Construction of a stereogram
    Cooperage
    Danger! Radioactive waste
    Dawn of the solar age: Solar energy
    Dawn of the solar age: Wind and water energy
    Digital technology (MM)
    Ductile materials (MM)
    Energy auditing in buildings
    Energy: Making things go (FS)
    Energy: What about tomorrow?
    The flame moves east
    Flere atomkraftvaeker (More nuclear power stations)
    Forging: The pivotal industry
    The future
    Harnessing the sun (FS)
    Hitler's secret weapon
    The hottest show on earth
    How to build an igloo
    If you can keep your cool
    Incident at Brown's Ferry
    Insulation story
    It's what's outside that counts (MM)
    Living with a limit: Practical ideas for energy conservation (MM)
    Look to the sun
    Meteosat
    Les meuniers de St–Eustache
    No act of God
    Now that the dinosaurs are gone
    Nuclear energy (set) (FS)
    Nuclear power (MM)
    Nuclear power (series) (FS)
    Nuclear power: Pro and con
    Nuclear reaction in Wyhl
    Onshore planning for offshore oil: Voices from Scotland
    Le pain d'habitant: La construction du four
    The paradox of plenty
    Pattern for engineering
    Pedal power
    Pencil
    Plastics (MM)
    Plastics (series) (FS)
    Polyurethanes: The versatile chemicals (MM)
    Project Sage
    Radiation and health
    Report from Rossing
    Science and you (series) (FS)
    Seabrook: Do we need it?
    Self portrait
    Solar energy: Ready when you are (MM)
    The solar frontier
    Solar heating

The solar quest (FS)
Solarex photovoltaic demonstration kit (MM)
The sound of danger
Sound: Recording and reproduction (set)
Sound: Recording and reproduction (set) (FS)
The story of great American inventors: How their inventions
    changed our lives (series) (FS)
Switch on the sun (rev. ed.)
Technical drafting (FS)
Technical drafting (MM)
Tell me please (series) (FS)
Teton: Decision and disaster
This nuclear age
Timber: The species for the job
Toast
Turn to the wind
Waterground
Ways to weld
We will freeze in the dark
The wells of Montrose
Windscale: Nuclear fuel recycling
Within this earth (FS)
TELEVISION see JOURNALISM AND COMMUNICATION
TRANSPORTATION AND DRIVER EDUCATION
    Auto repair: The costly ride
    Boats (MM)
    Les chars
    Drive and survive
    Gasoline and how to stretch it
    Going places (series) (FS)
    Hell Gate: The watery grave
    How to keep your Volkswagen alive (RT)
    How to overhaul a carburetor (series) (FS)
    Know your automobile (series) (FS)
    Motorcycle safety: Sharing the road
    Moving on
    Not like other ships
    Passenger problems on moving buses
    Pedal power (series) (FS)
    Railroads and westward expansion: 1800–1845
    Railroads and westward expansion: 1845–1865
    Ten–tenths ice
    Time to stop again
    Where shipwrecks abound
URBAN PLANNING see ARCHITECTURE AND URBAN
    PLANNING
VOCATIONAL AND TECHNICAL TRAINING
    The ABC of hand tools
    Bartending
    Building a model house (series) (FS)
    The control factor
    Die springs: Selection, use, maintenance
    Electric welding safety and set–up (FS)
    Fistful of power (set)
    Handling round timber
    How the motor car works – Part 2 – The carburettor
    How to use automotive precision tools (series) (FS)
    Office worker series (series) (FS)
    Portion control: A team effort
    Portion control: A team effort (FS)
    Portion control: A team effort (MM)
    Proofreading (MM)
    The reach truck cowboy
    Safe at work in plastics extrusion
    The safety and health of welders
    Transcription techniques (MM)
    Woodworking machine operations explained (series) (FS)
WOMEN see also WOMEN – HISTORY AND CONDITION OF
    WOMEN in MEDIAGRAPHY SECTION
WOMEN
    The American woman: A social chronicle (series) (FS)
    Beware the rapist
    By themselves
    A century of struggle and enterprising women (RT)
    Common sense self defence
    The doll factory
    EEO considerations: Interviewing women candidates (set)
    The Equal Rights Amendment: A simulation (MM)
    Folly (Bride and broom)
    Great grandmother

CLASSIFIED SUBJECT INDEX

FILMSTRIPS

Leonard Peck Prodns., 1977. si col $9.00
Two girls are on a train and experience a time warp which brings them to the year 1857. They become acutely aware of 20th century technology.
[Literature and drama] 1) Science fiction – Juvenile 2) Technology – Juvenile 813.0876 Gr 4–6
– Previews v6 n7, Mar, 1978. p13. Curran, N.E.

PHILADELPHIA AND VALLEY FORGE
see
THE LIVING SPIRIT OF '76 (SERIES)

PHILLIS WHEATLEY
see
WOMEN OF THE AMERICAN REVOLUTION (SERIES)

PHINEAS BUMBY'S PRESENT
see
BASIC SPELLING: PROBLEM WORDS (SERIES)

PHONETIC RULES IN READING (SET) (4 filmstrips)
(Series: Life Skills)
Singer/SVE, 1978. 50–55 fr ea 8–9 min ea sd col, 8 tests, 24 activity sheets, etc. $99.00 (w/cass)
Many of the words used as examples in this reading program are technical terms.
[Language arts and reading skills] 1) Reading – Phonetic method 374.012 Gr 9–Ad
+ Booklist v74 n20, Jun 15, 1978. p1630. Schmidt, K.
"A well–produced kit of high quality . . . "

PHOTOGRAPHIC COPYING
see
PRODUCING EFFECTIVE AUDIOVISUAL PRESENTATIONS (SERIES)

PHOTOGRAPHY
see
PRODUCING EFFECTIVE AUDIOVISUAL PRESENTATIONS (SERIES)

PHOTOGRAPHY (SERIES) (5 filmstrips)
Chicago Public School Art Society, 1977. 5–10 fr ea col $25.00
This filmstrip series offers examples of different types of photography and instructions on photographic and darkroom techniques.
[Photography] 1) Photography 771 Gr 4–12
+ Booklist v74 n12, Feb 15, 1978. p1020. Herbert, B.A.
"Perfect for both the novice and seasoned photography teacher . . . "
+ Previews v7 n3, Nov, 1978. p26. Barnes, S.

PHOTOSYNTHESIS
see
LIFE SCIENCES: THE PLANTS (SERIES)
THE SCIENCE OF PLANTS (SERIES)

PHYSICAL AND CHEMICAL CHANGES
see
EXPLORING MATTER AND ENERGY (SERIES)

PHYSICAL ASSESSMENT: EYE AND EAR (SERIES)
see
ASSESSING HEARING – ADULTS
ASSESSING HEARING – CHILDREN
ASSESSING THE FUNCTION OF THE EYE
EXAMINING THE EXTERNAL AND MIDDLE EAR
EXAMINING THE EXTERNAL EYE, PART I
EXAMINING THE EXTERNAL EYE, PART II
EXAMINING THE INTERNAL EYE

PHYSICAL CHANGES AND THEIR IMPLICATIONS
(Series: Perspectives on Aging)
Concept Media, 1973. 31 min sd col $70.00
This program on geriatrics examines the physical changes in the systems of the body.
[Health and medicine] 1) Aging 612.67 Gr Ad
* HosHealthPro v5 n3, 1978. p101. Davis, A.J.

PHYSICAL SCIENCE (SERIES) (3 filmstrips)
LIGHT
HEAT
SOUND
McGraw-Hill, 1977. 81–88 fr ea 17–18 min ea sd col $54.00 (w/cass)
Experiments demonstrate properties of light, heat, and sound.
[Physics] 1) Physics 530.4 Gr K–9
+ Previews v7 n2, Oct, 1978. p16. Gore, J.

THE PHYSICAL SCIENCES
see
BEGINNING CONCEPTS/SCIENCE (SERIES)

THE PHYSIOLOGIC IMPORTANCE OF HUMIDITY
see
INTRODUCTION TO RESPIRATORY THERAPY: UNIT I – HUMIDITY AND AEROSOL THERAPY: MODULE 3 – THE PHYSIOLOGIC IMPORTANCE OF HUMIDITY

PHYSIOLOGICAL DRIVES
see
WHY WE DO WHAT WE DO: HUMAN MOTIVATION (SERIES)

THE PHYSIOLOGY OF EXERCISE (SET) (1978)
+ Previews v6 n5, Jan, 1978. p16. DeLong, E.

PICK A PATTERN PICK A PATCH
see
PEOPLE WHO WORK, UNIT I (SET)

THE PICTORIAL LIFE STORY OF ANDREW JACKSON (SET)
(4 filmstrips)
(Series: Life Stories of Great Presidents)
Davco Publishers, 1977. 66 fr ea 13 min ea sd col $89.00 (w/cass)
Animation in the comic–book style tells the life story of Andrew Jackson, seventh President of the United States.
[Biography] 1) Jackson, Andrew, Pres. U.S. 2) U.S. – History – 1815–1861 923.173 Gr 5–10
+ Booklist v74 n10, Jan 15, 1978. p830. Kuehn, P.

THE PICTORIAL LIFE STORY OF ANDREW JOHNSON (SET)
(4 filmstrips)
(Series: Life Stories of Great Presidents)
Davco Publishers, 1977. 68 fr ea 13 min ea sd col $89.00 (w/cass)
Designed to enhance reading skills, this kit traces the life and political career of President Andrew Johnson.
[Biography] 1) Johnson, Andrew, Pres. U.S. 2) U.S. – History – 19th century 923.173 973.81 Gr 7–10
+ Booklist v74 n10, Jan, 15, 1978. p831. Greenspan, V.
" . . . this colorful kit achieves its goal with dramatic visuals and a clear, precise sound track."

THE PICTORIAL LIFE STORY OF DWIGHT D. EISENHOWER (SET)
(4 filmstrips)
(Series: Life Stories of Great Presidents)
Davco Publishers, 1977. 68 fr ea 13 min ea sd col $89.00 (w/cass)
This pictorial sketch of the life of Dwight D. Eisenhower covers his early life and highlights of his military and political career.
[Biography] 1) Eisenhower, Dwight David, Pres. U.S. 2) U.S. – History – 20th century 923.173 973.92 Gr 7–12
+ Booklist v74 n12, Feb 15, 1978. p1024. Gordon, A.
"Dramatic enough to hold the attention of a class and leave students waiting anxiously for the next part . . . "

THE PICTORIAL LIFE STORY OF GEORGE WASHINGTON (SET)
(4 filmstrips)
(Series: Life Stories of Great Presidents)
Davco Publishers, 1977. 68–74 fr ea 13 min ea sd col $89.00 (w/cass)
This filmstrip series recounts George Washington's life and career.
[Biography] 1) U.S. – History – 18th century 2) Washington, George, Pres. U.S. 923.173 973.3 Gr 5–9
+ Booklist v74 n8, Dec 15, 1977. p695. Fleming, M. "Whil visuals of the filmstrips match . . . the book, the projected images are superior to the printed ones."

THE PICTORIAL LIFE STORY OF THOMAS JEFFERSON (SET)
(4 filmstrips)
(Series: Life Stories of Great Presidents)
Davco Publishers, 1977. 68 fr ea 13 min ea sd col $89.00 (w/cass)
Flashbacks of Thomas Jefferson's life are juxtaposed with an account of the American Revolution and the Declaration of Independence.
[Biography] 1) Jefferson, Thomas, Pres. U.S. 2) U.S. – History – 18th century 923.173 973.3 Gr 5–11
+ Booklist v74 n8, Dec 15, 1977. p696. Bitely, J. "Students who have always found history dull and difficult will learn concrete, interesting facts in this kit . . . "

THE PIED PIPER OF HAMELIN
see
WORLD MYTHS AND LEGENDS (SERIES)

PIKE'S PEAK OR BUST!
see
GOLD FEVER: MIDAS ON A MULE (SET)

PIONEER WOMEN AND BELLES OF THE WILD WEST
see
THE AMERICAN WOMEN: A SOCIAL CHRONICLE (SERIES)

NICEM INDEXES

National Information Center for Educational Media
University of Southern California
Los Angeles, CA 90007

The National Information Center for Educational Media issues over a dozen indexes, some of them several volumes. Eight cover individual audiovisual formats. The rest combine entries from those volumes into multimedia indexes for specific disciplines or purposes. The indexes to filmstrips, overhead transparencies, motion cartridges, educational videotapes, audiotapes, records, and slides have been revised at approximately two-year intervals. This is another expensive reference set beyond the financial capacity of most school—or even district—media centers, but the media specialist who has access to a *current* set nearby will use it frequently for verification. It should be noted that each index and the entire set are available in microfiche at half the cost of the bound volumes. Consider purchase in that format, but only if nothing but title searches will be the intended use. Since subject searches in NICEM can be quite unsatisfactory (as further detailed below), microfiche would be a quite rational decision.

NICEM indexes, are comprehensive, aiming to list all titles for all ages in each format. Though they claim to be up to date, releases of up to two years prior to publication date may be missing. Out-of-print titles continue to be carried, however.

Listing in the body of each index is by title, and component segments in a set or series are entered under their own as well as under the series title—a unique and helpful feature. Each entry reveals exact format, running time, number of visuals, and release date. These are the data not generally supplied in vendor catalogs and without which it is impossible to do a conscientious job of selection.

The *Index to Educational Videotapes* can help ascertain film availability in video formats.

For a subject search in a NICEM index, the (alphabetical) Index to Subject Headings must be consulted first. This can identify the headings in the form and terminology employed here and where they may be found in the hierarchical structure of the subject section. That section is divided, in most of the indexes, into twenty-six categories, some with over 100 subcategories, arranged both in further hierarchical breakdowns, and alphabetically within those. Since the Index to Subject Headings has no cross-references, it is important to look up any term that can possibly have any relevance.

An example may make this clearer: In looking for videotapes on energy, "energy" in the Index to Subject Headings mentions: "Science—Physical—Basic Physical Science—Energy and Matter," "Science—Physics—Energy and Matter," and "Social Science—Resources—Energy." Checking further under "Power" reveals "Social Science—Resources—Power" and also "Industrial and Technical Education—Engines and Power Systems." "Solar energy" retrieves two more references ("Industrial and Technical Education—Engines and Power Systems—Solar Engines" and "Social Science—Resources—Solar." To make sure no relevant subject headings are missed, it makes good sense to also check the Subject Heading Outline at the very beginning of each volume, which in turn refers to "Social Science—Resources—Coal" and others.

Perhaps the only thing this discussion makes clear is how cumbersome it is to try to identify media on a given subject through these indexes. And, after finally finding the desired heading(s), the user is then faced with a list of media often many columns long and with no dates indicated. This throws the user back to attempting to make choices from likely sounding titles. Out-of-print and extremely dated materials are listed along with current ones, without distinction. Grade levels are indicated, however. Nevertheless, relevant titles may be missed. The search for energy materials missed *The House That NASA Built*. That documentary was entered in "Industrial and Technical Education–Construction, Building"–properly so, but with no indication that what was constructed was a prototype energy-efficient house. The Index to Subject Headings takes up eighteen pages in the *Index to Educational Videotapes*, but even so it lacked the terms "coal," "solar heating," and "synthetic fuels."

The amount of flipping back and forth required in the process just described is cumbersome in softcover volumes. It is beyond endurance with microfiche. (That is why these indexes are recommended in fiche format for title searches only.) The shorter indexes consisting of just one volume, i.e., those for overhead transparencies, 8mm motion cartridges, videotapes, audiotapes, records, and slides, are a bit less frustrating to use than the multivolume ones for films and filmstrips.

The publishers promise four *Updates* to purchasers of the complete set of indexes in either hardcopy or on microfiche. These are arranged similarly, with separate sections for media in each format. Since the *Updates* access the most recent materials, subject searching could be restricted to them, or they could at least be consulted initially.

Figure 10 on page 104 shows the number of titles in the various NICEM indexes. Sample pages of NICEM indexes are reproduced on pages 105 through 109. (Reprinted by permission of National Information Center for Educational Media.)

FIGURE 10–NUMBER OF TITLES IN NICEM INDEXES

INDEX	NUMBER OF TITLES		
	1977 ed.	1980 ed.	Additions (Deletions)
16mm Educational Films	100,000	100,000	0
35mm Educational Filmstrips	70,000	75,000	5,000
Educational Overhead Transparencies	5,000	5,800	800
8mm Motion Cartridges	26,000	22,000	(4,000)
Educational Videotapes	15,000	16,000	1,000
Educational Audiotapes	28,000	28,000	0
Educational Records	25,000	28,000	3,000
Educational Slides	28,000	37,000	9,000
TOTAL	297,000	311,800	14,800

Index to
EDUCATIONAL
VIDEOTAPES

NATIONAL INFORMATION CENTER FOR EDUCATIONAL MEDIA (NICEM)

UNIVERSITY OF SOUTHERN CALIFORNIA

UNIVERSITY PARK

LOS ANGELES, CALIFORNIA 90007

Fifth Edition (1980)

Fingerpainting
B 15 min
2 INCH VIDEOTAPE K
Teaches a form of creative self-expression in which the feeling of body, arm and hand movements are translated onto paper. (Broadcast quality) From The Roundabout, Unit 4 Series.
Prod-WETATV Dist-NITC

Finishing And Decorating
C 29 min
2 INCH VIDEOTAPE
Features Mrs Vivika Heino introducing and demonstrating the basic techniques for finishing pottery and decorating it. From The Exploring The Crafts - Pottery Series.
Prod-WENHTV Dist-PUBTEL

Finishing Touch, The (And Fashion Show)
C 29 min
2 INCH VIDEOTAPE
See series title for descriptive statement. From The Designing Women Series.
Prod-WKYCTV Dist-PUBTEL

Finishing Up
C 29 min
2 INCH VIDEOTAPE
See series title for descriptive statement. From The Busy Knitter II Series.
Prod-WMVSTV Dist-PUBTEL

Finishing, Occlusal Correction, Insertion, And Adjustment
C 13 min
3/4 INCH VIDEO CASSETTE PRO
Shows how relief and adjustment of critical areas of the framework and saddles of the removable partial denture will contribute to the continued oral health of the oral tissues. Presents areas requiring modification and occlusal adjustments by both laboratory remounting and direct check bites. Issued in 1967 as a motion picture. From The Removable Partial Dentures, Clasp Type - Clinical And Laboratory Procedures Series.
LC No. 79-706178
Prod-USVA Dist-USNAC 1978

Finite Systems
B 30 min
2 INCH VIDEOTAPE T
Shows examples of finite mathematical systems. Reviews the definition of a mathematic field and introduces the idea of a group. (Broadcast quality) From The Sets And Systems Series.
Prod-WETATV Dist-OPRINT

Fire
C 15 min
2 INCH VIDEOTAPE
Follows a rookie fire fighter as he learns about handling a pumper and hose. Emphasizes that practice helps the firemen meet the crisis when a hose bursts at a fire. From The Ripples Series.
LC No. 73-702132
Prod-NITC Dist-NITC

Fireboat - Ready For A Run
C 13 min
3/4 INCH VIDEO CASSETTE P-I
Describes the services, many different pieces of equipment, duties and training of a fireboat crew through a viewing of an actual fireboat run.
Prod-AIMS Dist-AIMS 1968

Fireman
B 15 min
2 INCH VIDEOTAPE K
Introduces the fireman and shows the special clothes and equipment he needs to do his job. Illustrates the procedure for reporting a fire by means of a fire alarm box. (Broadcast quality) From The Roundabout, Unit 1 Series.
Prod-WETATV Dist-NITC

Fireman - On Guard
C 11 min
3/4 INCH VIDEO CASSETTE P-I
Presents a capsule account of the many duties of firemen and how children can be of help.
Prod-AIMS Dist-AIMS 1963

Fireman, Fireman
C 15 min
2 INCH VIDEOTAPE P
Shows the activities and responsibilities of a fireman from battling a blaze to caring for his uniform and equipment. From The Words Are For Reading Series.
Prod-MAETEL Dist-NITC 1972

Fireman, The
C 10 min
2 INCH VIDEOTAPE K
Assists children in oral language development by introducing the fireman and the importance he plays in the community. From The Rhyme Time Series.
Prod-DETPS Dist-OPRINT

Fires Of Creation - A Series
Features John Burton, an artist in glass, presenting his ideas on art and philosophy.
Prod-KCET Dist-PUBTEL
Fires Of Creation, Pt 1 29 min
Fires Of Creation, Pt 2 29 min
Fires Of Creation, Pt 3 29 min

Fires Of Creation, Pt 1
C 29 min
2 INCH VIDEOTAPE
See series title for descriptive statement. From The Fires Of Creation Series.
Prod-KCET Dist-PUBTEL

First Day In Kindergarten, A
B 30 min
2 INCH VIDEOTAPE P-I
See series title for descriptive statement. From The Kindergarten Development In The Kindergarten Series.
Prod-GPITVL Dist-GPITVL

First Dimension - Information And Understanding
C 60 min
2 INCH VIDEOTAPE P A
Deals primarily with the delivery of facts and attitudes on drug abuse as a basis for further dialogue on the problem. Includes a history of drug use, statistics on the spread of drugs today, the physiological effects of a number of these drugs and a montage of prevailing attitudes toward drug abuse. From The Turned On Crisis Series.
Prod-WQED Dist-GPITVL

First Films On Science - A Series
P-I
Prod-MAETEL Dist-NITC 1975
Changes In Classes Of Energy 15 min
Changes In Kinds Of Energy 15 min
Chemical Changes In Matter 15 min
Energy And Motion 15 min
Mass And Volume 15 min
Matter 15 min
Matter Is Made Of 15 min
Measurement 15 min
Physical Changes In Matter 15 min
Solar Energy 15 min

First Forty Days, The
C 24 min
3/4 INCH VIDEO CASSETTE
Deals with the first 40 days of American combat in Korea, including the arrival of troops, unloading supplies and equipment, combat, blowing up bridges and establishing defense lines. Issued in 1950 as a motion picture.
LC No. 79-706643
Prod-USA Dist-USNAC 1979

First Impact, The
C 52 min
3/4 INCH VIDEO CASSETTE J-C A
Presents a record of one immigrant's sojourn in the United States. Features Alistair Cooke's memoir of how I came to America and the people, places, institutions and landscapes that I admired enough to make me want to stay. From The America - A Personal History Of The United States Series. No. 12
LC No. 74-701583
Prod-BBCTV Dist-TIMLIF 1972

Marriage Game, The, Pt 1   C 45 min
3/4 INCH VIDEO CASSETTE
Describes Elizabeth I's romance with the Earl of Leicester, whom she eventually tries to match up with her cousin, Mary, Queen of Scots. From The Elizabeth R Series No. 2.
Prod-BBCTV   Dist-TIMLIF   1976

Marriage Game, The, Pt 2   C 45 min
3/4 INCH VIDEO CASSETTE
Describes Elizabeth I's romance with the Earl of Leicester, whom she eventually tries to match up with her cousin, Mary, Queen of Scots. From The Elizabeth R Series No. 2.
Prod-BBCTV   Dist-TIMLIF   1976

Marrieds, The   C 29 min
2 INCH VIDEOTAPE
Presents an interview with a 13-year-old girl and her mother. Includes problems of staying out late at night and other misbehavior. From The Counseling The Adolescent Series.
Prod-GPITVL   Dist-GPITVL

Mars - Is There Life   C 15 min
3/4 INCH VIDEO CASSETTE
Discusses the possible history of Mars and its present surface topography of volcanoes, ice caps and canyons. Discusses the Viking lander and its biology experiments in relation to the search for life on Mars.
LC No. 78-706267
Prod-NASA   Dist-USNAC   1978

Mars - The Search Begins   C 29 min
3/4 INCH VIDEO CASSETTE
Examines the planet Mars, using pictures taken by the Mariner 9 spacecraft.
LC No. 79-706058
Prod-NASA   Dist-USNAC   1979

Mars And Beyond   C 15 min
3/4 INCH VIDEO CASSETTE
Deals with the Viking Mission to Mars to explore the biochemical components of life. Demonstrates the chemical conditions involved and discusses the potential significance of the biochemical findings in relation to theories concerning Martian life.
LC No. 78-706265
Prod-NASA   Dist-WHROTV   1978

Marshes Of 'Two' Street, The   C 29 min
2 INCH VIDEOTAPE
See series title for descriptive statement. From The Synergism - In Today's World Series.
Prod-KVIETV   Dist-PUBTEL

Marshlands - Where The Action Is   C 20 min
2 INCH VIDEOTAPE
Examines the interrelationships and interdependencies of plants and animals within the marsh community. Suggests improving marshland management. From The Natural Science Specials Series. Module Green
Prod-UNPRO   Dist-NITC   1973

Marxism   B 45 min
2 INCH VIDEOTAPE
See series title for descriptive statement. From The Social Science, No. 2 Series. Unit 3 - Conflicting Political Ideals Of Today
Prod-CHITVC   Dist-OPRINT   Prodn-WITWTV

Marxist Economics And The Planned Economy   B 29 min
2 INCH VIDEOTAPE   C A
Reviews Marxist criticism of the market economy and describes the planned economy in Russia and China today, noting its advantages and its inefficiencies. From The Economics And The Public Interest, Economics I Series.
Prod-WGBHTV   Dist-NITC   1967

Mary   B 30 min
2 INCH VIDEOTAPE
Presents an interview with a 13-year-old girl and her mother. Includes problems of staying out late at night and other misbehavior. From The Counseling The Adolescent Series.
Prod-GPITVL   Dist-GPITVL

Mary Kingsley   C 52 min
2 INCH VIDEOTAPE
Dramatizes Mary Kingsley's 1893 journey along the Ogowe and Rembwe Rivers of Africa's West Coast, where she studied the native cultures of the cannibalistic tribes. From The Ten Who Dared Series.
LC No. 77-701579
Prod-BBCTV   Dist-TIMLIF   1976

Masculine And Feminine (French)   C 14 min
2 INCH VIDEOTAPE   H-C A
Presents two humorous sketches involving the opposite sexes. From The En Francais Series. Part 2 - Temporal Relationships, Logical Relationships
Prod-MOFAFR   Dist-NITC   1970

Mask, The   B 33 min
3/4 INCH VIDEO CASSETTE
Describes how alcohol may mask symptoms of both physical and mental disorders. Suggests a system of observation used by the police and general public in detecting the signs of alcoholism.
Prod-USNAC   Dist-USNAC   1972

Masks   B 20 min
2 INCH VIDEOTAPE
Shows how masks can delight or frighten the observer and how they can be made from a variety of materials, including papier-mache, paper bags, or by paper sculpture. From The For The Love Of Art Series.
Prod-GWTVAI   Dist-GPITVL   Prodn-WETATV

Masks - Art About Us   B 20 min
2 INCH VIDEOTAPE   P
See series title for descriptive statement. From The Art About Us Series.
Prod-NCCSTV   Dist-OPRINT   Prodn-KFMETV

Masks - Time For Art   B 20 min
2 INCH VIDEOTAPE
See series title for descriptive statement. From The Time For Art Series.
Prod-NCCSTV   Dist-OPRINT   Prodn-KFMETV

Mass And Energy   C 30 min
2 INCH VIDEOTAPE   J
Shows that mass is equivalent to energy, but that it can be converted in appreciable quantities only by the special techniques of fission and fusion. From The Nature Of Matter, Pt 3 - Energy Series.
Prod-MPATI   Dist-OPRINT

Mass Transportation   B 20 min
2 INCH VIDEOTAPE   I-J
See series title for descriptive statement. From The Crossroads Series.
Prod-SDITVA   Dist-SDTVA   1967

Mass 1 - The Case Of The Disappearing Mass   C 15 min
3/4 INCH VIDEO CASSETTE   I-J
Presents a girl and a famous retired French detective who solve the mystery of a disappearing mass, an elephant, using metric measurement. Demonstrates milligrams, grams, kilograms and tonnes. From The Measurement Series.
LC No. 77-700911
Prod-AIT   Dist-AIT   1977

Mass 2 - The Case Of The Disappearing Mass   C 15 min
3/4 INCH VIDEO CASSETTE   I-J
Presents a girl and a famous retired French detective solving the mystery of a disappearing mass, an elephant, using metric measurement. Demonstrates milligrams, grams, kilograms and tonnes. From The Measurement Series.
LC No. 77-700911
Prod-AIT   Dist-AIT   1977

Masseter And Temporal Muscles   C 14 min
3/4 INCH VIDEO CASSETTE   PRO
Presents the anatomy of the lateral aspect of the head, including deep dissection views of the muscles, tissue spaces and associated nerves and vessels of the temporal and masseter areas. From The Anatomy Of The Head And Neck Series.
LC No. 78-706249
Prod-USVA   Dist-USNAC   Prodn-VADTC   1978

Messing A Window   C 30 min
2 INCH VIDEOTAPE
See series title for descriptive statement. From The Making Things Grow II Series
Prod-WGBHTV   Dist-PUBTEL

Master Spy Of The Revolution   B 30 min
2 INCH VIDEOTAPE   I-J
Tells the spying activities of Paul Revere and visits his home in Boston. Hosted by Mr Salelan. From The Let's See America Series.
Prod-NET   Dist-NITC

Mastering Basic Math Skills, Unit A - Fractions – A Series   I-H
Prod-MVNE   Dist-TELSTR   1973
Adding Like Fractions   10 min
Adding Like Mixed Numbers   12 min
Adding Unlike Fractions   15 min
Adding Unlike Mixed Numbers   9 min
Basic Fractions
Common Denominators   13 min
Comparing Fraction Sizes   8 min
Dividing Fractions   15 min
Dividing Mixed Numbers   11 min
Equivalent Fractions   13 min
Equivalent Fractions - Multiplying And...   18 min
Mixed Numbers And Improper Fractions   23 min
Multiplying Fractions, A   9 min
Multiplying Fractions, B   19 min
Multiplying Mixed Numbers   11 min
Reducing Fractions   9 min
Subtracting Like Fractions   11 min
Subtracting Like Mixed Numbers   11 min
Subtracting Unlike Mixed Numbers   8 min

1 ENERGY
Science - Physical
Basic Physical Science - Energy And Matter
Physics - Energy And Matter

2 Basic Physical Science - Energy And Matter

About Energy (I)	NITC
Are All Stars Alike (P)	GPITVL
Atom And Current Electricity, The (I)	GPITVL
Atom And Static Electricity, The (I)	GPITVL
Atoms (J)	GPITVL
Atoms And Their Fundamental Particles (I)	GPITVL
Basic Units Of Matter (J)	VRCOA
Big Bang, The	TIMLIF
Bottom Of The Oil Barrel, The (I A)	NITC
Changes In Classes Of Energy (P-I)	NITC
Changes In Kinds Of Energy (P-I)	GPITVL
Changes In The State Of Matter (P)	NITC
Chemical Changes in Matter (P-I)	AIMS
Cold (P-I)	GPITVL
Colors (K)	GPITVL
Condensation (P)	
Conditions Relating To The Physical State Of Matter (P)	GPITVL
Electrical Appliances (J)	GPITVL
Electron Movement (J)	GPITVL
Element, The - Atomic Number And Weight - Isotopes (I)	
Energy - Ability To Do Work (P-I)	AIMS
Energy And Motion (P)	GPITVL
Energy And Motion (P-I)	NITC

3 Physics - Energy And Matter

Atoms (J)	GPITVL
Basic Units Of Matter (J)	GPITVL
Big Bang, The	VRCOA
Bottom Of The Oil Barrel, The (I A)	TIMLIF
Cohesion - Adhesion	PUBTEL
Crab Nebula, The (H-C A)	TIMLIF
Dawn Of The Solar Age - Solar Energy (H-C A)	TIMLIF
Dawn Of The Solar Age - Wind And Water Energy (H-C A)	TIMLIF
Determination Of The Formula Of A Compound (H-C)	SAUNDW
Electrical Appliances (J)	GPITVL
Electron Movement (J)	GPITVL
Expansion And Contraction (J-H)	NITC
Experimenting With Electricity (J)	GPITVL
Generating Electricity Chemically (I)	GPITVL
Heat Transfer (I)	NITC
Investigating The World Of Science, Unit 1 Matter And Energy - Introduction (J)	GPITVL

4 Resources - Energy

Challenge Of The Future	USNAC
Energy - The American Experience	USNAC
Geothermal - Nature's Boiler	USNAC
House That NASA Built, The	USNAC
Sun Power For Farms	USNAC
There's Coal In Them Thar' Hills	TIMLIF
They Call The Wind Energy	UMICH
Transportation - The Way Ahead	USNAC
Ultimate Energy, The	USNAC
What Price Coal	WGBHTV

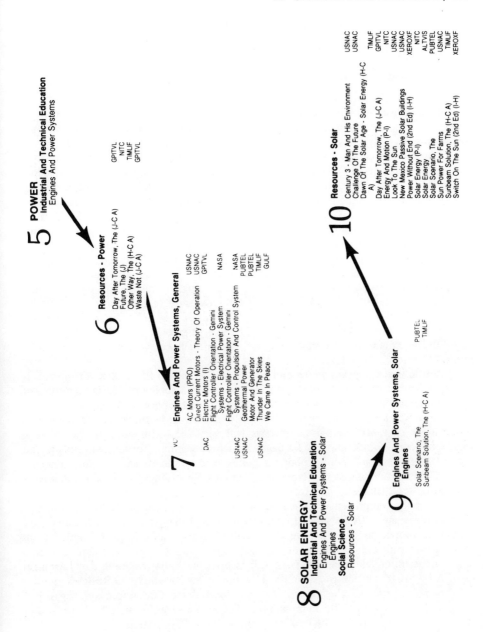

5 POWER
Industrial And Technical Education
Engines And Power Systems

6 Resources - Power

Day After Tomorrow, The (J-C A)	GPITVL
Future, The (J)	NITC
Other Way, The (H-C A)	TIMLIF
Waste Not (J-C A)	GPITVL

7 Engines And Power Systems, General

AC Motors (PRO)	USNAC
Direct Current Motors - Theory Of Operation	USNAC
Electric Motors (I)	GPITVL
Flight Controller Orientation - Gemini Systems - Electrical Power System	NASA
Flight Controller Orientation - Gemini Systems - Propulsion And Control System	NASA
Geothermal Power	PUBTEL
Motor And Generator	PUBTEL
Thunder In The Skies	TIMLIF
We Came In Peace	GULF

8 SOLAR ENERGY
Industrial And Technical Education
Engines And Power Systems - Solar
Engines
Social Science
Resources - Solar

9 Engines And Power Systems, Solar Engines

Solar Scenario, The	PUBTEL
Sunbeam Solution, The (H-C A)	TIMLIF

10 Resources - Solar

Century 3 - Man And His Environment	USNAC
Challenge Of The Future	USNAC
Dawn Of The Solar Age - Solar Energy (H-C A)	TIMLIF
Day After Tomorrow, The (J-C A)	GPITVL
Energy And Motion (P-I)	NITC
Look To The Sun	USNAC
New Mexico Passive Solar Buildings	USNAC
Power Without End (2nd Ed) (I-H)	XEROXF
Solar Energy (P-I)	NITC
Solar Energy	ALTVIS
Solar Scenario, The	PUBTEL
Sun Power For Farms	USNAC
Sunbeam Solution, The (H-C A)	TIMLIF
Switch On The Sun (2nd Ed) (I-H)	XEROXF

SCHOOL LIBRARY JOURNAL

New York: Bowker, 1954- . Monthly (except June and July).
$32.00/yr. (Publisher's address: R. R. Bowker, 1180 Avenue
of the Americas, New York, NY 10036.)

"Audiovisual Review" is a regular feature of this journal, published ten times
a year (no June or July issues). Under the editorship of the former editor of *Previews*,
this section partially fills the void left by that magazine's cessation.

The section carries from forty-five to fifty reviews per issue, approximately a
third of what a typical *Previews* issue contained. Reviews are signed and are by school
media specialists, Instructional Materials Center directors, and, on occasion, faculty
members or subject specialists from schools of education. The articles critique content, technical quality, pacing, and, more rarely, the quality of the teacher's guide.
Usage suggestions generally conclude the evaluations, many of which reflect testing
with students. Lack of recommendation may be openly stated or implied.

The bulk of the reviews are for filmstrips and films and videocassettes, with a
few added ones for slides, kits, and spoken recordings. They are arranged by medium,
and the film-and-video and filmstrip categories are further divided into subject group-
ings. Subject categories are ad hoc and flexible, contrary to the practice of *Booklist*
and other selection aids which employ standard lists of subject headings. This practice
facilitates the retrieval of materials on newly emerging concerns such as "life skills,"
"special education," or "energy sources." No one subject area is emphasized over
others.

A title index appears at the end of the section, and a title index for the year is
in the December issue. The April 1982 issue featured a survey of media on a topic of
current interest, a practice which had been an important service of *Previews*.

Since *School Library Journal* is already in place in learning centers as a prime
professional tool, its audiovisual reviews will very likely function as the primary
source for current information. Its pages are worth scanning for announcements and
reviews of professional publications, including mediagraphies, and for recommendations of ALA committees of "Notable Children's Recordings," "Notable Children's
Filmstrips," or "Selected Films for Young Adults."

The only comprehensive overview of current audiovisual production is afforded
by this magazine's "AV Forecast," the September 1981 issue of which noted 762
series and individual titles projected for fall 1981 and early 1982. Compiled from
information supplied by distributors, each entry supplies physical and contents
descriptions, intended grade level, as well as price and other ordering data. Arrangement is by broad subject areas, similar to those of the "Audiovisual Review" section.

Sample pages of the *School Library Journal* are reproduced on pages 111
through 113. (Reprinted by permission of *School Library Journal*, April 1981, and
March 1981, p. 119. R. R. Bowker Company/A Xerox Corporation.)

for children's, young adult, and school librarians

SCHOOL LIBRARY JOURNAL

ISSN 0362-8930

APRIL 1981

National Library Week, Apr. 5-11

slj /AUDIOVISUAL/ REVIEW

Editor-in-Chief: Lillian N. Gerhardt
Audiovisual Editor: Phyllis Levy Mandell

16mm Films & Videocassettes

ENERGY SOURCES

Generation on the Wind. 16mm or videocassette. color. 26 min. with tchr's. guide. Prod. by Windmill Movie Co. Dist. by Churchill Films. 1979; 1980 release. $430. Preview avail. Catalog kits.
Gr 7 Up—Advocates of small scale technology may enjoy this film which chronicles the evolution of a large wind generator on the island of Cuttyhunk, located some 14 miles off the New England Coast. Built by a group of amateurs, the construction seems as much a response to a unique challenge as it is an effort to provide the 50 island residents with electrical power which would bypass their Diesel generators. The film is a montage of construction sounds and interviews with project personnel and island residents interspersed with a minimal narrative. The visual quality is good. There is limited discussion of windmills (with appropriate Dutch visuals) and some personal comments about alternate technology. There are no comments of the intricacies of the project development or how much electricity was finally provided and at what cost. However, the film is interesting as a testimony to what a group of enthusiastic neophytes can accomplish.—*George A. Sands, Jr., Caroline County Public Library, Denton, Md.*

ENVIRONMENT & ECOLOGY

Island at the Edge. 16mm or videocassette. color. 26 min. with tchr's. guide. Prod. by Hardy Jones Prods. Dist. by Films Inc. 1979; 1980 release. 16mm: $425 (Rental: $50); videocassette: $255. Preview avail.
Gr 9 Up—The hundreds upon hundreds of dead and dying dolphins lying in bloodied waters near the island of Iki, in Japan, were reported on by the media following their slaughter by Japanese fishermen in 1978 and again in 1979. This film's producer, along with a group of environmentalists, went to Iki to investigate and found a situation "far more complicated than the world's press had portrayed." His camera focused on a beautiful, prosperous society whose existence depends on fishing and is threatened by a diminishing catch. Interviews with local fishermen and the Buddhist priest alternate with scenes of fishing for yellowtail and squid and attempts by sound engineers to use sonic discouragers to dispel the dolphins competing for the catch. The film succeeds in its objectives—to examine a culture whose economic base is being destroyed by modernization, to raise the level of awareness of the fishermen and alert them to the fact that "the problems at Iki originate not with dolphins but with man, with pollution, and with overfishing. Recommended for students of environmental sciences and journalism and for those conservationists concerned with the preservation of marine mammals.—*Frances M. Volz, Long Island University, Greenvale, N.Y.*

GUIDANCE—GENERAL

The Myths of Shoplifting. 16mm or videocassette. color. 16 min. with tchr's. guide. Prod. by National Retail Merchants Assn. Dist. by Churchill Films. 1980. $295. Preview avail. Catalog kit.
Gr 7 Up—This dramatic film, realistically presented by male and female actors, shows students that shoplifting is a crime with extreme consequences.

The first episode shows a young woman drop a wallet into her shoulder bag, leave a store, and drive off in a convertible. She brags to a friend that it is easy to shoplift and that it does not really hurt anybody. At this point, the shot freezes for a moment while the narrator explains that this is myth number one about shoplifting. Five more misconceptions are pointed out which show that shoplifting is a crime which can change one's life. The youngster who might be tempted to steal on a dare could possibly be deterred by having seen this film.—*Karlan Sick, George Washington Junior High School, Alexandria, Va.*

Shoeshine Girl. 16mm or videocassette. color. 30 min. with tchr's. guide. Prod. by McDonald Prods. Dist. by Learning Corporation of America. 1980. LC 79-701411. $425 (Rental: $40). Preview avail.
Gr 4-9—Sarah's parents send her to spend the summer with an aunt in a small town after they find some shirts in her drawer that they didn't buy. Forced to earn money, she takes a job with the town's shoeshine man and has a special learning and growing summer. The technical qualities of the film are excellent. The story moves well and holds viewers' interest. What makes this film special is the characterizations presented by the actors. Tammy Grigas, as Sarah, has just the right pout, just the right amount of change in attitude to make it believable. The film is based on the book by Clyde Robert Bulla (Crowell, 1975) and would certainly encourage students to read the book. It will be most useful in values clarification discussions.—*Mary Michener, Lincoln Elementary School, Ellensburg, Wash.*

Sarah takes a job as a "Shoeshine Girl" for the summer (Learning Corp. of America)

SCIENCE BOOKS AND FILMS

Washington, DC: American Association for the Advancement of Science, 1965- . 5x/yr. $17.50. (Publisher's address: American Association for the Advancement of Science, 1515 Massachusetts Avenue, NW, Washington, DC 20005.)

This journal, long known for its carefully crafted reviews of books and films, instituted equally authoritative reviews of filmstrips with its 1980/1981 volume. Its scope extends to social science subject areas, such as anthropology, geography, planning, social services, and psychology, as well as to all aspects of pure and applied science. It thus nicely complements *Booklist*, which reviews relatively few science titles. The magazine is issued five times each year with approximately twenty reviews per issue.

Reviews here are in Dewey Decimal order and rate programs as "highly recommended" (**), "recommended" (*), "acceptable" (Ac), or "not recommended" (NR). They also indicate the level of difficulty, from K (Kindergarten and Preschool) to P (Professional). These designations are supported by signed one-paragraph critiques.

The film review section includes an occasional review of a videocassette, but availability of 16mm films in video formats is not indicated.

The annual index in the May/June issue lists (by distributor) titles reviewed during the year.

Media centers can save several times the annual subscription price of *Science Books and Films* by having it on hand for regular consultation of all of its review sections (books, films, filmstrips) by both media specialist and teaching staff. A search for current science materials will most profitably start in its pages.

SOCIAL STUDIES SCHOOL SERVICE

10,000 Culver Boulevard
Culver City, CA 90230

"We believe our books, filmstrips and other supplementary materials are the best and most effective available," states the catalog of this jobber for instructional materials in social studies and ancillary subjects. Building-level media, including simulation games, are found among the books and workbooks which make up the bulk of the offerings. The free secondary catalog, issued annually, covers topics from business education to world history. Separate catalogs, also free, are available for some of these subjects and for intermediate-junior high grades (4-9).

Arrangement is quite random within each of these topics, but is aided by a combined title and subject index. Entries for each item give rather full descriptions, detailing subject coverage, contents of kits, etc. They omit the frame count or running time of filmstrips or their individual titles, and not all of them provide copyright or release dates. That particular omission makes it difficult to judge how current a title might be, even given its presumed quality.

The wise buyer should check other sources before purchasing expensive items from this catalog. Previewing is only possible at the company's California showroom (or at conventions)—which are hardly suitable locations to conduct a careful evaluation. A return privilege is offered, however, for materials in "salable" condition.

Before ordering a set of four filmstrips for $80, the purchaser needs to at least know the titles of each and have a bit more information than six lines of copy. The order numbers used by this distributor include a producer code that is not difficult to divine; in other cases, the producer's name is supplied. One can thus turn to the producer's catalog to glean more data, possibly references to reviews. Checking in the *NICEM Index to Filmstrips*, if available (see pp. 102-103), may reveal dates and format details. Checking in *Media Review Digest* may disclose critical recommendations.

Many single filmstrips costing from $20 to $30, and even less expensive games, sets of posters, or study prints, are offered here. At that price range, the buyer can certainly feel free to select items without extensive checking or previewing.

Sample pages of the Social Studies School Service catalog are reproduced on pages 116 through 120. (Reprinted by permission of Social Studies School Service.)

TEACHER RESOURCE MATERIALS
PAPERBACK

THE NEWSPAPER: An Alternative Textbook. By J. Rodney Short and Bev Dickerson. The newspaper is, these authors claim, the ideal secondary classroom textbook. Socially relevent, geared for low-level readers, and informative on a wide range of subjects, the newspaper contains features (sports, entertainment, important news events) that interest even the reluctant reader. This guide for teachers analyzes the newspaper from front page to classified ads, explaining how to use it to study a wide range of social studies topics, as well as journalistic vocabulary and writing style. Activities are provided that require students to read the paper carefully and research and write items of their own. Glossary. Pitman Learning. 117 p. © 1980.
FEA101-11 $5.50

SOUND FILMSTRIPS

STUDENT MOTIVATION SERIES. Lively filmstrips in this classroom-oriented series are designed to stimulate the learning potential of low achievers. Comprehensive teacher's guides include objectives, presentation suggestions, and filmstrip scripts. Grades 6-12. Pentagram. © 1978.
COMPLETE SERIES OF 2 PROGRAMS:
PTG100-11   8 color filmstrips, 8 cassettes, 2 guides $176.00

STUDENT SELF-IMAGE AND STUDY MOTIVATION. The development of each student's potential is encouraged in four fundamental areas: improving self-image, setting goals, creating good study habits, and developing classroom learning skills. Among other things, students learn about the incredible brain, the development of their real potential, the rewards of understanding, how to enjoy studying, and the value of effort and persistence.
PTG011-11   4 color filmstrips, 4 cassettes, guide $94.00

BASIC APTITUDE DEVELOPMENT. Four fundamental areas are covered in this program of four filmstrips: mastering the basics (reading, writing, math, and art), improving mental abilities (such as perception, memory, and reasoning), being motivated rather than discouraged by low grades, and preparing for tests. The filmstrips cover such things as avoiding math fear, strengthening weaknesses, increasing intelligence and self-confidence, being "teachable," and avoiding test paralysis.
PTG021-11   4 color filmstrips, 4 cassettes, guide $94.00

DUPLICATING MASTERS

BASIC TOOLS FOR THE SOCIAL STUDIES TEACHER. Includes book report form, research report form, guide for answering essay questions, guide for making an outline, guide for locating social studies material in the library, guide for reading your daily newspaper, basic social studies vocabulary, key dates in American History, national and world leaders, countries of the world, outline maps of the world and the United States.
CEBH11-11   20 spirit duplicating masters $7.95

PAPERBACKS

BUILDING MOTIVATION IN THE CLASSROOM. By Robert C. Hawley and Isabel L. Hawley. The aim of this book is to help classroom teachers cover their academic subjects and motivate student learning at the same time. It presents a detailed, structured sequence of classroom motivational techniques with over 100 suggestions for establishing a positive learning climate. These suggestions include having students interview their teacher, sharing emotions, building support for risk-taking, developing learning flow charts with students, brainstorming as a means of teaching classification, and using student self-evaluation forms. A useful tool for teachers at all levels. 8½" x 11". Education Research Associates. 114 p. © 1979.
ERA10-11 $9.95

SURVIVAL KIT FOR TEACHERS (AND PARENTS). By Myrtle T. Collins and DWane R. Collins. An alphabetically arranged dictionary and guidebook for discipline and behavior problems in the classroom. The authors present 324 different cross-referenced student behaviors from abrasiveness, anxiety, and argumentativeness to truancy, wastefulness, and withdrawal. Over 1,000 options are suggested to aid teachers in coping with these behaviors. Under each title, the student behavior is briefly outlined with a list of recommended alternative teacher reactions to each behavior. Teacher resource. Goodyear. 223 p. © 1975.
GDY882-11 $10.95

For more teacher resource materials, see pages 229, 230, 242 and 243.

TABLE OF CONTENTS

INDEX

MULTICULTURAL STUDIES

SOUND FILMSTRIPS

THIS IS MINE: The Ethnic Dilemma. The United States is experiencing a resurgence of ethnic identity. This sound color filmstrip examines the period of change from "melting pot" to pluralism and how it has affected the social roles of such peoples as Blacks, Mexican-Americans, Native Americans, and Puerto Ricans. Teaching Resources/New York Times. ©1975. Suitable for upper elementary and secondary students.

NYT991R	1 color filmstrip, 1 LP record, teacher's guide	**$22.00**
NYT991C	1 color filmstrip, 1 cassette, teacher's guide	**$22.00**

THE OTHER MINORITIES. A brief study of the American Indian, Mexican-American, Cuban, Puerto Rican, and Oriental minorities in America, through both historical and contemporary perspectives. The program shows how minority groups seek to achieve a part in the mainstream of American life without sacrificing their own heritage. The program is useful in grades 6-9 and for slower moving classes in high school and adult school. New York Times. ©1972.

NYT410R	1 color filmstrip, 1 LP record, teacher's guide	**$22.00**
NYT410C	1 color filmstrip, 1 cassette, teacher's guide	**$22.00**

ETHNIC FOODS. A brief survey of the foods from all over the world which have been integrated into American diets, from hotdogs to wonton soup. The filmstrip shows how ethnic groups have maintained their unique foods while entering the mainstream of American life in others areas. The method of preparation of some foods, including tacos and Chinese stir-fried vegetables, are described. Educational Design. ©1973.

EDS64C	1 color filmstrip, 1 cassette, teacher's guide	**$26.00**

JAPANESE AMERICANS: An Inside Look. The history, contributions, and hardships of the Japanese in America, as told through the eyes of a Japanese American woman. Traces Japanese immigration, the development of legal and social discrimination, and the World War II detention camp experience. The narrator, through her personal experience, emphasizes the rights of all U.S. citizens, regardless of origin. Teacher's manual includes an outline of the program, lesson ideas, and an extensive bibliography. Grades 4-8. Multi-Media Productions.

MM6017R	2 color filmstrips, 1 LP record, teacher's guide	**$20.00**
MM6017C	2 color filmstrips, 1 cassette, teacher's guide	**$20.00**

THE IRISH EXPERIENCE. A 12-year-old Irish immigrant boy describes his experiences on the streets of New York in the 1850's, the prejudice against Irish, the struggle of his railroad-worker father to survive, the poor housing available, and the corrupt politics of Tammany Hall. Multi-Media Productions.

MM6012R	1 color filmstrip, 1 LP record, teacher's guide	**$15.00**
MM6012C	1 color filmstrip, 1 cassette, teacher's guide	**$15.00**

Send for your free copy of our **MULTICULTURAL CATALOG** for a complete listing of our materials on ethnic studies, prejudice, and human relations.

INDIVIDUALIZED READING

ETHNIC READING SERIES. High interest, low reading level series contains biographies of famous people from various ethnic groups. In each booklet the text is followed by an exercise section that helps student build vocabulary and comprehension skills. The concept level of the stories is mature while reading level is maintained at the fourth grade level. The booklets are sold in sets of 10 of the same title in a package. Book Lab.

ETHNIC READING SERIES: JEWISH AMERICANS. By Irving Gerber.

BLB4614	Haym Salomon: Patriot of Liberty, set of 10	**$6.75**
BLB4615	Emma Lazarus: Poet of Liberty, set of 10	**$6.75**
BLB4616	George Gershwin: The Music Man, set of 10	**$6.75**
BLB4617	Albert Einstein: World Scientist, set of 10	**$6.75**

ETHNIC READING SERIES: ITALIAN AMERICANS. By Irving Gerber and Ida S. Meltzer.

BLB4618	Mother Cabrini: Missionary to the World, set of 10	**$6.75**
BLB4619	Joe DiMaggio: The Yankee Clipper, set of 10	**$6.75**
BLB4620	Fiorello H. LaGuardia: The Little Flower, set of 10	**$6.75**
BLB4621	Arturo Toscanini: Genius of Conducting, set of 10	**$6.75**

SOUND FILMSTRIPS

OUR MULTI-ETHNIC HERITAGE. Five sound color filmstrips introduce students to the contributions of five different ethnic groups who immigrated to the United States in the 19th and 20th centuries. Each filmstrip examines the history of the immigration, the problems each group faced, the areas in which they settled, the contributions they have made to American life, and the most famous Americans of that group. Each filmstrip is accompanied by a 6-page teacher's guide which includes the script, discussion questions, vocabulary, and a bibliography. Upper elementary and junior high grades. Educational Activities. ©1976.

1. Chinese-Americans
2. Irish-Americans
3. Italian-Americans
4. Jewish-Americans
5. Scandinavian-Americans

EAC463R	5 color filmstrips, 5 LP records, 5 teacher's guides	**$84.00**
EAC463C	5 color filmstrips, 5 cassettes, 5 teacher's guides	**$84.00**

PAPERBACKS

AN ILLUSTRATED HISTORY OF THE CHINESE IN AMERICA. By Ruthanne Lum McCunn. An exploration of the lives of Chinese immigrants to this continent, from earliest times to the present. The text, accompanied by over 100 period photographs, gives an account of how the Chinese, often treated as second class citizens, have emerged since World War II as important individuals in American politics, law, science, and the arts. A free teacher's guide includes teaching suggestions, questions, and answers. Appropriate for students in grades 5-12. Design Enterprises of San Francisco. 133 p. ©1979.

DEF802-20	1-4 copies $6.95 each
	5 copies and over $6.25 each

REMEMBER THE DAYS: A Short History of the Jewish American. By Milton Meltzer. An account of the Jews in America, from the scattered Jewish settlers of colonial days to Zionism and contemporary militance. Particular emphasis is put upon the 19th and 20th century migration from central and eastern Europe, and Jewish life in America at the turn of the century. Illustrated. Reading level: Grade 6. Zenith. 114 p. ©1974.

DD04-20	1-4 copies $2.50 each
	5 copies and over $2.00 each

THE JEWISH FESTIVALS: History and Observance. By Hayyim Schauss. A history of the origins and evolutions of the Jewish holidays, including discussions of how celebrations differ from country to country. The rituals, ceremonial objects, utensils, foods, and prayers are described for the Sabbath, Pesach, Rosh Hashonah, Yom Kippur, Sukkos, Chanukkoh, Purim, and others. Schocken. 316 p. ©1938. 1975 paperback edition.

SCK413-20	1-4 copies $4.95 each
	5 copies and over $4.45 each

GETTING TO KNOW THE VIETNAMESE AND THEIR CULTURE. By Vuong G. Thuy. This book seeks to inform Americans about Vietnamese customs, education, religious beliefs, and characteristics. The author, a Vietnamese-born educator who lives in the United States, stresses the influence of family devotion, politeness, and morality on Vietnamese behavior, and discusses some of the difficulties to be expected as this group merges into 20th century American life. Frederick Ungar. 94 p. ©1976.

FUP905-20	1-4 copies $3.95 each
	5 copies and over $3.60 each

PRODUCER CATALOGS

Although the great bulk of book purchases for libraries can be made from jobbers and wholesalers, that is not the case with audiovisual media where the generally greater expense and fewer reviews make previewing a necessity. The services of the one major wholesaler active in the audiovisual field have been described (pp. 71-74). Preview prints are more readily obtained from producers or distributors, and audiovisual materials are thus often bought directly.

For that reason, a file of current catalogs is a must in the resource center (in addition to those of the three distributors singled out on pages 67, 71, 115). The catalogs must be used with caution and supplemented, whenever possible, with objective data.

Few such catalogs tell copyright or production dates or the length or number of frames for each filmstrip. (For exceptions, see figures 11 and 12 on pages 122 and 123.) None give details about teachers' guides. These are essential pieces of information if the user does not want to waste time viewing a skimpy strip—or one that's too lengthy for a young audience. Without knowing the copyright date, a user might pick a title on oceanography dating to the 1950s or one on environmental problems dating to 1970.

Most catalogs feature new releases, however, either listing them separately, noting them in the index, or marking them with special symbols. (Several that do not are noted in figure 14, page 123.) "New programs" are generally releases of the current year and up to three years old; those four to five years old are not distinguished from others that may have been completed up to ten or fifteen years earlier. The most recent materials are also generally displayed at exhibits.

It should be noted that a program marked "new" in a catalog may be new only to the particular distributor and may have been produced for another firm four or five years earlier. Verification in the appropriate NICEM index may uncover such a discrepancy. If so, the user will certainly want to check previous reviews, using *Media Review Digest*, and consider whether the subject matter has remained unchanged over the five-year period and whether the manner of presentation has remained timely. If a major function of filmstrips and other small media is to update textbooks (see p. 18), that function obviously cannot be well served other than by truly current programs.

Most media specialists, knowing their school's needs, will certainly scan the "new releases" portion of each catalog coming across their desks, marking likely titles for possible preview. As was said above, it pays to check these reviews in *Media Review Digest* first. Scanning current catalogs is the way to keep abreast of current production, along with referring to *School Library Journal*'s "AV Forecast" and *Library Journal*'s "AV Showcase" (pp. 92-93, 110). To ensure receiving a flow of such current catalogs, media centers should be on the mailing lists of many firms.

Selectors welcome catalogs that display dates and places of reviews of older programs (see figure 11, page 122). They are particularly well disposed toward producers whose products carry CIP (Cataloging in Publication) data. This practice caught on with such speed and directness in the publishing industry that it is truly puzzling why the same universality could not be achieved in the media industry. To find release dates of older programs, a quick check of the title indexes in the appropriate *Core Collection* or the *Elementary School Library Collection* can pay off. If these are unavailing, the appropriate NICEM index may reveal date and length of the program. If the copyright or release date is within reason and the length satisfactory in relation to price, a preview may then be requested. If convenient,

Media Review Digest may be checked for reviewers' recommendations. Many programs are, of course, never reviewed.

Sales personnel can be expected to provide copies of reviews for older programs and field test data for both older and newer programs.

Vendor catalogs are important for obtaining data for titles that initially come to the media specialist's attention through a favorable review or a catalog, such as those of the Children's Book and Music Center (p. 67) or the Social Studies School Service (p. 115). These sources may omit titles of individual filmstrips in a set, along with exact scope of contents or intended grade levels. A review may not note the order number or indicate whether segments are available separately, as will some catalogs (figure 13, page 123). The price will often have changed.

Distributors of 16mm films are responding to the widespread interest in video formats, and many of them offer to supply all their programs in such formats. Institutions looking to video for economy will be disappointed, however. The price is often the same as that for film. Many distributors permit recording on users' equipment for a fee, and this may be financially more attractive. This text only calls attention to nonprofit video distributors (see pp. 55-62, 82-86).

FIGURE 11—PRODUCER CATALOGS SUPPLYING PRODUCTION, RELEASE, OR REVIEW DATES FOR ALL OR SOME PROGRAMS*

Bergwall
Bobbs-Merrill
Center for Humanities
Centron
Clearvue
Coronet
Creative Learning
EMC
Educational Images
Encore
Enjoy Communicating
Eye Gate
Hawkhill
Human Relations Media
Ibis
Imperial Educational Resources
January
Learning Corporation of America

Library Filmstrip Center
Lyceum
McGraw-Hill
Marshfilm (LC number)
Math House
Moody (LC number)
National Geographic
Orange Cherry
Pathescope
Polished Apple
Pomfret House
Science and Mankind
Social Studies School Service
Society for Visual Education
Sunburst Communications
United Learning
Visual Education Corporation

---

*Distributors are asked to supply corrections to these lists compiled from 1980 and 1981 catalogs.

FIGURE 12—PRODUCER CATALOGS SUPPLYING FORMAT DATA
(Frame Counts and/or Running Times)*

Barr
Bergwall
Center for Humanities
Clearvue
Crystal
Encore
Encyclopaedia Britannica
Films Inc.
Focus Media
Hawkhill
Ibis
International Film Bureau
Learning Corporation of America
Library Filmstrip Center

Lyceum
Marshfilm
Media Fair
Moody
Multimedia Productions
Outdoor Pictures
Perfection Company
Polished Apple
Pomfret House
Science Software Systems
Society for Visual Education
Visual Education Corporation

FIGURE 13—PRODUCERS SELLING PARTS OF FILMSTRIP SETS SEPARATELY*
(Replacement Parts Are Available from Some Others)

Bergwall
Clearvue
Coronet
Creative Visuals
Crystal
Educational Audiovisual
Educational Enrichment Materials

Eye Gate
Hubbard
International Film Bureau
Learning Tree
Peller
Pomfret
Society for Visual Education

FIGURE 14—PRODUCER CATALOGS SUPPLYING NO IDENTIFICATION OF
NEW RELEASES*

Ampersand
Barr
Brady
CMS Records
Creative Visuals
Crystal
Denoyer
EMC
EMI
History Simulations
International Film Bureau

Interpretive Education
Media Basics
Moody
Nystrom
Prentice-Hall Learning Systems
Q-Ed
Spoken Arts
Troll
United Transparencies

---

*Distributors are asked to supply corrections to these lists compiled from 1980 and 1981 catalogs.

ART MUSEUMS

A wealth of materials is available from museums, among them slide programs at far less cost—and probably of better quality—than similar programs from educational producers. It would be well to be on the mailing lists of the art museum nearest one's school and those of two or three leading museums as well, perhaps the National Gallery of Art and the Metropolitan Museum of Art, and be alerted to their resources for the teaching of art and ethnic and area studies.

Sources for Mediagraphies

An up-to-date, well-prepared mediagraphy (a listing of audiovisual media on a given topic, corresponding to a bibliography) can be the best starting point in selection work. Finding one that fits that description is not easy, however. When found, each mediagraphy must be used differently, depending on whether it is critical or not. Both critical and noncritical listings have their place in selection work, provided the exact nature of each list used is understood. For critical guides, the evaluation criteria employed in compilation should be known. Other factors to note include grade level and the completeness of data provided. It is important to note the cut-off date of any published mediagraphy. In the time it takes to compile and publish one, such a guide could become a year or more out of date. Nonetheless, updating it, using the selection tools described earlier in this volume, is considerably easier than starting "from scratch." Here are places to look for mediagraphies.

PROFESSIONAL JOURNALS

Professional journals in various disciplines occasionally publish such recommended lists. Teachers reading those journals (e.g., *Music Educator's Journal*, *Social Education*, *American Biology Teacher*, and others) should certainly bring such lists to the media center director's attention, as they would do with reviews of single titles which might possibly be added to the center's collection. (Both mediagraphies and reviews are indexed in *Media Review Digest*, but only much later.)

Previews

New York: Bowker, 1972-1980. (Publisher's address: R. R. Bowker, 1180 Avenue of the Americas, New York, NY 10036.)

Between September 1978 and December 1980, when it ceased publication, *Previews* featured mediagraphies in most of its issues. They are tabulated in figure 15, page 126, with the caveat that they will be seriously dated in just a few years and must be brought up to date. But they can be recommended for retrospective searches, expecially where the selection of a number of titles on a subject is contemplated. Some are selective; others are quite comprehensive rosters of available materials. All are arranged for easy scanning and provide details on format, number of visuals, running time, and some indication of content.

FIGURE 15–MEDIAGRAPHIES IN *PREVIEWS*

Title	Selective	Descriptive	Date	Grades
Aging and the Aged: A Multimedia Roundup		x	2/80	
Basic Photography and Film-making Techniques		x	12/80	
Bright Ideas for Consumer Education: A Recommended Multi-media Collection	x		9/79	
Career Awareness for the Elementary Grades: A Multimedia Collection		x	3/80	elem.
Career Education Media	x		11/78	
Children's Novels on Film			5/79	elem./middle
China: Past, Present, and Future: A Multimedia Collection		x	12/79	
Death Education: A Retrospective Mediagraphy			10/79	
Drug and Alcohol Use and Abuse; A Recommended Media Collection	x		1/80	sec.
Energy for Tomorrow: Today's Crisis and Future Sources		x	11/79	
Family Violence: Battered Children and Women		x	10/80	sec.
Folktales and Legends in Children's Films	x		9/78	elem.
Holiday Celebrations throughout the Year: A Mediagraphy for Elementary Grades			9/79	elem.
How to Develop Better Study Habits and Test-Taking Skills		x	11/80	
Juvenile Crime and Its Consequences; A Recommended Media Collection	x		4/80	
Media for Consumer Health Care: A Recommended Collection	x		10/79	
Media for Library Skills Instruction	x		1/79	
A Media Menu: Nutrition for Elementary Grades			2/80	elem.
The Presidency and the Electoral Process: A Multimedia Roundup		x	9/80	
Safety for Elementary Grades: A Multimedia Roundup		x	5/80	elem.
Selected Media for Special Education	x			
Sex Education: Media for Elementary Grades		x	1/80	elem.
A Tautology of Short Story Films	x		2/79	sec.

Curriculum Review

Chicago: Curriculum Advisory Service, 1960- . 5x/yr. $35.00.
(Publisher's address: Curriculum Advisory Service, 500 South Jefferson,
Chicago, IL 60607.)

The author's "Media Monitor" column in this journal surveys five times yearly the recent and recommended media on timely topics. It generally briefly describes from twenty-five to forty selected titles in the text, and supplies ordering data at the end of the column. The magazine consists chiefly of in-depth reviews, grouped by curriculum area, of texts, resource units, books for students and teachers, and an increasing number of audiovisuals. Each issue focuses on one or more topics, often interdisciplinary, besides addressing the major curriculum divisions (language arts, mathematics, science, social studies). The featured topic is the subject of the "Media Monitor" column (earlier title "Media Notes"). (For past column topics, see the table of contents below.)

Between 1977 and 1980, the author also published a newsletter, *Media Monitor*, which surveyed resources on discrete topics (see below). A one-volume edition of the entire *Media Monitor* run, supplemented by *Curriculum Review* columns through November 1981, was published as *The Complete Media Monitor* (Scarecrow, 1981).

THE COMPLETE MEDIA MONITOR

Table of Contents

MEDIA MONITOR

MEDIA NOTES

TEACHERS' GUIDES

Teachers' guides, teachers' editions of texts, and professional references in various disciplines will frequently carry lists of additional readings or suggested resources. The media manager needs to know what is being suggested (and what, as a result, the media center may be asked to supply). Finding this out also creates the opportunity to inform teachers of alternative resources already in the center or available for purchase. Resource guides of this nature should always be checked for recency, quality, and selectivity, and *not* used blindly as buying guides.

SCHOOL AND STATE SOURCES

Large city and county school districts, and some state departments of instruction, issue lists of approved learning materials. Similar guides may be part of adopted curriculum guides. The rule in each jurisdiction will determine whether buying must be entirely from such approved lists or whether they are meant as suggestions only.

BOOKS AND PAMPHLETS

Mediagraphies in hardcover or pamphlet form are published from time to time. Recent ones have addressed materials for sports, women's studies, economics, area studies, and others. Such publications are regularly announced or reviewed in library/ media professional journals. The columns of *Booklist, Media and Methods, School Library Journal, Wilson Library Bulletin*, and of teachers' magazines should be followed for such announcements.

ERIC

Mediagraphies published in ERIC are most readily found by scanning the listings under publication types 051 (Guides—Classroom Instructional Materials, for learners), 052 (Teaching guides, for teachers), and 131 (Bibliographies), if machine searching is not available.

REFERENCES

Corcoran, Frances, and Blickle, Calvin. *Sports Materials*. Neal-Schuman, 1979. 245p.

Harter, Charlotte T. *Audiovisual Materials for Teaching Economics*. 3rd ed. Joint Council on Economic Education, 1980. 160p.

Nordquist, Joan. *Audiovisuals for Women*. McFarland & Co., Jefferson, NC: 1980. 145p.

Sive, Mary R. *The Complete Media Monitor*. Scarecrow Press, 1981. 196p.

Wilson, Cathy R., and Schug, Mark C. *A Guide to Games and Simulations for Teaching Economics*. 3rd ed. Joint Council on Economic Education, 1979. 85p.

PART III

Previous portions of this text outlined the general principles of media selection in anticipation of instructional situations, and listed the publications that can furnish the required information. This portion will look at the same information with a view to recommending the most efficient procedures for current and retrospective searches for various formats. This discussion will be followed by specific examples from various subject areas and instructional stages that reflect availability and prices in the fall of 1981.

Search Strategies

Figure 16 calls attention to the essential sequence that is advocated here:

FIGURE 16—EIGHT STEPS IN MEDIA SELECTION

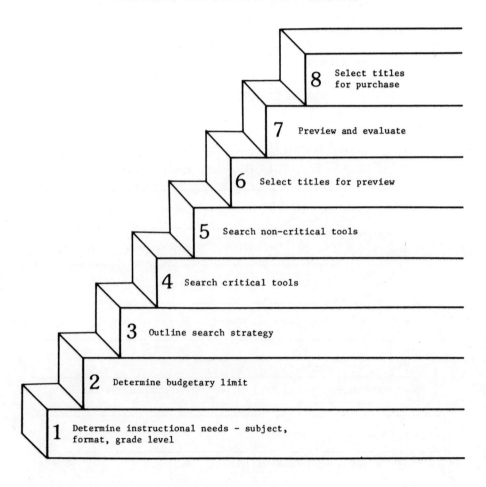

8   Select titles for purchase

7   Preview and evaluate

6   Select titles for preview

5   Search non-critical tools

4   Search critical tools

3   Outline search strategy

2   Determine budgetary limit

1   Determine instructional needs - subject, format, grade level

It is recommended that a search of critical tools always be made before referring to noncritical sources. This procedure is followed in the examples in chapter 13. Figures 8 and 9 on pages 53-54 identify both critical and noncritical current and retrospective tools. Fitting this process into steps 4 and 5 of figure 16 produces the two types of searches outlined in figures 17 and 18. Each of these searches is in effect a subset of steps 3 to 5 of figure 16. Note that retrospective searches offer more options for critical appraisals than current searches.

That total dependence on critical tools is an unattainable ideal is demonstrated by the examples in chapter 13. Like all ideals, it is no less worth pursuing for that reason. The reviewing journals—*Booklist, School Library Journal,* and *Science Books and Films*—among them assess no more than a fraction of current audiovisual output. But it must also be recognized that not all critical reviews are equally reliable, nor are all noncritical descriptions without merit. Reviewers may get overly enthusiastic about an appealing show without regard to its instructional potential, or lack of it. The selector needs the objective data supplied by a noncritical source such as the appropriate NICEM catalog. Such data are a bit harder to extricate from the promotional prose of vendor catalogs.

FIGURE 17—CURRENT SEARCHES

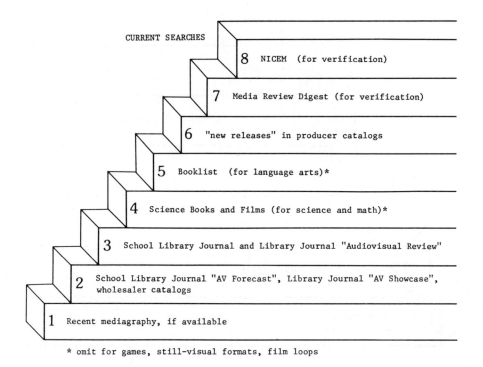

CURRENT SEARCHES

8 NICEM (for verification)

7 Media Review Digest (for verification)

6 "new releases" in producer catalogs

5 Booklist (for language arts)*

4 Science Books and Films (for science and math)*

3 School Library Journal and Library Journal "Audiovisual Review"

2 School Library Journal "AV Forecast", Library Journal "AV Showcase", wholesaler catalogs

1 Recent mediagraphy, if available

* omit for games, still-visual formats, film loops

FIGURE 18—RETROSPECTIVE SEARCHES

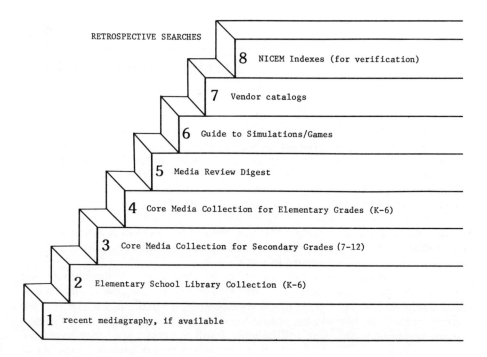

RETROSPECTIVE SEARCHES

8   NICEM Indexes (for verification)

7   Vendor catalogs

6   Guide to Simulations/Games

5   Media Review Digest

4   Core Media Collection for Elementary Grades (K-6)

3   Core Media Collection for Secondary Grades (7-12)

2   Elementary School Library Collection (K-6)

1   recent mediagraphy, if available

13
Examples: Problem-Solving

The examples in this chapter provide scenarios which apply the suggestions of earlier chapters to specific problem-solving situations. These involve needs identified or requests made by teachers, media specialists, administrators, and students. Based on actual and hypothetical sets of facts, each example starts with a statement of the problem, noting objectives, target audience, preferred format, etc. Next follows the strategy to be employed, including budgetary limits. "Preliminary Selection" notes the selection aids consulted and results obtained, generally in a combination of retrospective and current searches. The resolution of the problem is described in the final portion. Most examples are accompanied by an illustration of a fully or partially answered form of the sort suggested in part I.

The six randomly selected examples in this chapter should demonstrate that judicious use of selection aids pays off. In not one of the cases could equally useful selections have been made simply by examining a handful of catalogs or a few convention exhibits. Nor was the process very difficult in any of the cases. The procedures suggested in this text will become almost automatic after they have been followed a few times. Shortcuts or other improvements may present themselves in the process.

If the selection process outlined here is followed, the resultant collection will be one that can satisfy the demand of the instructional development process. The teachers served will be able to find instructional materials for specific uses that will serve the purpose better than any others. Funds will be spent to their best advantage and waste will be avoided. The approval rating of the library/media center should see a healthy increase and its staff take satisfaction in improved performance.

EXAMPLE NO. 1 (TEACHER-INITIATED)

PROBLEM   Fifth-grade teachers discern that students who read below the level of the social studies text have trouble meeting the course requirements, which include learning the characteristics of each region of the United States.

STRATEGY $100 can be found in the teachers' combined budgets. The media specialist will identify no more than five programs that seem promising and assemble them for simultaneous previewing.

PRELIMINARY SELECTION

1. Critical sources

Browsing through the 917.3 and following sections of the *Elementary School Library Collection* turns up:

>*Focus on America* (SVE, 1972);
>
>*Seeing the American States* (Coronet, 1972-1975); and
>
>*Midwest* (United Learning, 1977).

All are priced way over the budgeted amount.

Core Media Collection for Elementary Grades yields:

>**Regions of America* (Learning Tree, 1974) and
>
>**Regions of the United States* (Troll, 1977).

Next, the Classified Subject Indexes of *Media Review Digest* for 1978 and 1979 call attention to:

>*U.S. Regional Studies* (Educational Dimensions, 1976).

2. Noncritical sources

The catalog of Charles W. Clark Co. lists two high-priced sets which are disregarded, and

>**United States Regional Geography* (Educational Dimensions, 1976),

apparently the same set as that retrieved through *Media Review Digest*.

Social Studies School Service carries

>*Regions of the United States* (United Learning, n.d.).

A check of the United Learning catalog reveals that set to be quite old, and *Midwest*, noted above, not to be part of a set or series.

The media specialist now turns to current catalogs, checking their "new releases" sections, and discovers

> *Panorama: These United States* (Educational Enrichment, 1980. $172.00; $24.00 each).

**FINAL
SELECTION**

The four sets marked * appear worth previewing, although all exceed the budgeted amount. Three of them, however, are available for partial purchase, and a decision to buy four or five strips rather than an entire set is a possibility.

Forms and worksheets for this example follow below and on pages 137 through 140.

NEEDS ASSESSMENT FORM

SUBJECT OR TOPIC regions of the U.S.		BUDGETED AMOUNT $100		
OBJECTIVES	Cognitive see Curriculum Guide	Affective		Motor
INSTRUCTIONAL LEVEL(S) Grade 5, RL 3-4		STUDENT CHARACTERISTICS below average readers		

EXPECTED USAGE Media Center _____ Number of Students ___15-20___

  Classroom ____x____ Length of Time _____all year_____

  Date Needed ____9/81____

DESIRED ATTRIBUTES	Visual x	Audio	Projection	Color x	Motion
HOW ORIGINATED	Teacher ____x____ Student _____		Administrator _____ Media Specialist _____		

SELECTION WORKSHEET

Set	Title	Size ## of pages ## of frames	Running Time	Contents Remarks*
917.3	REGIONS OF AMERICA	appr. 39 each	6-7 min.	location and characteristics
	Knowing and living in the Northeast			of region
Segments	" " South			living there
	" " Midwest			
	" " on the Great Plains			
	" " in the Rocky Mountain Region			
	" " " Pacific Region			

Tchr's guide __x__
Producer __Learning Tree #LT430__   Distributor _____   Grade level __K-6__
Release date __1974__   Format __6 fs. & cass.__   Price __$156__

Source	Date	Page	Remarks*
Producer			check current price, segments available separately?
Clark			
Ch.Ctr.			
SSSS			
Core Coll.	1978	180	Previews 9/75, U.S.-Description and Travel
ESLC			
MRD			
Horn			
SLJ			
Sci.Bks			
Booklist			
NICEM			
Other (name)			Our adopted text recognizes 8 regions

Abbreviations:

Ch.Ctr.	Children's Book and Music Center
ESLC	Elementary School Library Collection
Horn	Guide to Simulations/Games
MRD	Media Review Digest
SSSS	Social Studies School Service
Sci.Bks.	Science Books and Films

*Record here quotes, references to alternative titles,
other considerations for selection decisions

SELECTION WORKSHEET

Title / Set	Size ## of pages ## of frames	Running Time	Contents Remarks*
917.3 REGIONS OF THE U.S.	average 67	avge. 13	lifestyles, work
New England			geography,
Middle Atlantic States			resources,
Southeast			character of the
Midwest			American people
North Central States			
South Central "			

Tchr's guide X   Rocky Mountain States; Western and Pacific States

Producer Troll	Distributor	Grade level 4-9
Release date 1977	Format 8 fs. & cass.	Price $128; $16 each

Source	Date	Page	Remarks*
Producer	1980	25	approved by Baltimore, Los Angeles School Districts
Clark			
Ch.Ctr.			
SSSS			
Core Coll.	1978	181	917.3 U.S. - Geography, Booklist 1/15/78
ESLC			
MRD			
Horn			
SLJ			
Sci.Bks			
Booklist	1/15/78		
NICEM			
Other (name)			

Abbreviations:
Ch.Ctr.	Children's Book and Music Center
ESLC	Elementary School Library Collection
Horn	Guide to Simulations/Games
MRD	Media Review Digest
SSSS	Social Studies School Service
Sci.Bks.	Science Books and Films

*Record here quotes, references to alternative titles, other considerations for selection decisions

SELECTION WORKSHEET

917.3 Set	Title	Size ## of pages ## of frames	Running Time	Contents Remarks*
U.S. REGIONAL GEOGRAPHY		50–58	8 – 15	note separate unit on Alaska and Hawaii
Segments	The Northeast: Land of Supercity C 5341			
	The South: Land of Growth C 5342			
	South Central and Southwest: Opportunity C5343			
	Lake States: Farms and Industry C5344			
	North Central States: Plenty C5345			
	West: Rugged Beauty C5346			

Tchr's guide	Pacific States: C5347; Hawaii & Alaska C 5348		
Producer	Educ.Dimensions C5340CA	Distributor	Grade level 7–12
Release date 1976	Format 8 fs. & cass.		Price $160;$20 each

Source	Date	Page	Remarks*
Producer	1980	27	
Clark	81/82	225	land, people, style, economics, history; similarities and differences
Ch.Ctr.			
SSSS			
Core Coll.			
ESLC			
MRD	1978	402	Previews 11/77 p.20
Horn			
SLJ			
Sci.Bks			
Booklist			
NICEM			
Other (name)			

Abbreviations:

Ch.Ctr.	Children's Book and Music Center
ESLC	Elementary School Library Collection
Horn	Guide to Simulations/Games
MRD	Media Review Digest
SSSS	Social Studies School Service
Sci.Bks.	Science Books and Films

*Record here quotes, references to alternative titles, other considerations for selection decisions

SELECTION WORKSHEET

Set	Title	Size ## of pages ## of frames	Running Time	Contents Remarks*
Segments	PANORAMA: THESE UNITED STATES			
	The New England States #52384			
	The Middle Atlantic " 52385			
	The South Atlantic " 52386			
	The Middle Western " 52387			
	The South Central " 52388			
	The North Central " 52389			

Tchr's guide The Rocky Mountain States #52390, The Western & Pacific States #52391

Producer Educ.Enrichment #60057 | Distributor | Grade level 4-8

Release date 1980 | Format 8 fs. & cass. | Price $172;$24 each

Source	Date	Page	Remarks*
Producer	1981	59	diversity, natural forces & human needs, national parks
Clark			
Ch.Ctr.			
SSSS			
Core Coll.			
ESLC			
MRD			
Horn			
SLJ			
Sci.Bks			
Booklist			
NICEM			
Other (name)			

Abbreviations:

Ch.Ctr.	Children's Book and Music Center
ESLC	Elementary School Library Collection
Horn	Guide to Simulations/Games
MRD	Media Review Digest
SSSS	Social Studies School Service
Sci.Bks.	Science Books and Films

*Record here quotes, references to alternative titles,
other considerations for selection decisions

EXAMPLE NO. 2 (MEDIA SPECIALIST-INITIATED)

PROBLEM The media specialist notes a fairly recent (January 1980) mediagraphy of recommended drug and alcohol abuse materials (in *Previews*, see page 126 above) and decides to check the college's collection relating to alcohol abuse. The purpose is to see whether anything of exceptional value is missing.

STRATEGY Involve the health sciences instructors in this selection exercise for their subject expertise and knowledge of instructional needs and to encourage use both of the existing collection and of any additional materials acquired.

**PRELIMINARY
SELECTION** The mediagraphy lists eight videocassettes, six filmstrip sets, and two charts on alcohol topics. Among the cassettes are two free-loan programs from an agency of the U.S. Department of Health and Human Services.

The media center already owns one of the filmstrip sets (dated 1972). When the annotations for the others are compared, it is noted that the most high priced of the newer releases presents cartoon caricatures exclusively; another one lacks a teacher's guide. A sound-slide program released in 1978 turns out to actually be a reissue of a 1976 filmstrip set at little over half the cost, which indeed sounds quite promising.

A check of the starred (*) items in the Charles W. Clark catalog reveals no additional 1979 or later titles.

The media specialist makes marginal notes as needed, marks the ten most likely programs, and asks one of the health teachers to read the list. That individual advises that the health department already owns the two charts. Together they choose three programs to preview.

**FINAL
SELECTION** The health teachers preview the programs, using an evaluation form supplied by the media specialist. The media specialist in the meantime discovers a 1962 black-and-white filmstrip set among the center's holdings and discards it. The consensus after previewing is that the existing collection meets instructional needs, and no further purchases are necessary.

A form for this example follows on page 142.

NEEDS ASSESSMENT FORM

SUBJECT OR TOPIC alcohol abuse – evaluate existing collection			BUDGETED AMOUNT to be determined		
OBJECTIVES	Cognitive x		Affective x		Motor
INSTRUCTIONAL LEVEL(S) Human Services Program			STUDENT CHARACTERISTICS all		

EXPECTED USAGE	Media Center _____	Number of Students _300___
	Classroom __x___	Length of Time ___?___
	Date Needed _?___	

DESIRED ATTRIBUTES	Visual	Audio	Projection	Color	Motion

HOW ORIGINATED	Teacher _____ Student _____	Administrator _____ Media Specialist __all__

EXAMPLE NO. 3 (STUDENT REQUEST)

PROBLEM The media specialist notes that students have a demonstrated extra-curricular interest in psychology, a subject not taught in this particular high school, and at the same time notes a number of new programs on such topics in producer catalogs. If one can be found, a program on different schools of psychology would see much use in the media center. It should supplement books and lend some degree of concreteness to a quite abstract (and essentially nonvisual) subject.

STRATEGY The media center has a small fund, donated in memory of a student leader tragically killed, for the purchase of materials illustrating "leadership." Ask the student advisory committee helping to administer this fund to join in previewing and deciding whether the selected psychology program is an allowable purchase.

PRELIMINARY SELECTION

1. Critical sources

Core Media Collection for Secondary Schools lists

> *Landmarks in Psychology* (Human Relations Media, 1976).

A search in *Media Review Digest* is fruitless.

Science Books and Films for March-April 1981 reviews

> *New Pathways in Psychology* (Human Relations Media, 1980. $99.00),

terming it "highly recommended."

2. Noncritical sources

The Charles W. Clark catalog discloses

> *Basic Concepts in Psychology* (Prentice Hall Media). No date is given.

A close examination of the catalog of Human Relations Media, a producer that specializes in psychology materials, results in no additional leads.

No programs are shown in the catalogs of the Agency for Instructional Television or the Great Plains National Instructional Television Library.

FINAL SELECTION This is accomplished after simultaneous previewing of the three programs identified through the preliminary process.

Forms and worksheets for this example follow on pages 144 through 146.

NEEDS ASSESSMENT FORM

SUBJECT OR TOPIC
psychology -various schools, theories,
  leading names
		BUDGETED AMOUNT
		  to be determined		

OBJECTIVES	Cognitive x		Affective	Motor

INSTRUCTIONAL LEVEL(S)
  grades 11-12
		STUDENT CHARACTERISTICS
		  academic, college-bound		

EXPECTED USAGE	Media Center ___ x ___	Number of Students _40-50_
	Classroom _____	Length of Time _____
	Date Needed _____	

DESIRED ATTRIBUTES	Visual x	Audio x	Projection	Color	Motion
HOW ORIGINATED	Teacher _____ Student _____		Administrator _____ Media Specialist ___ x ___		

SELECTION WORKSHEET

Title Set	Size ## of pages ## of frames	Running Time	Contents Remarks*
150 NEW PATHWAYS IN PSYCHOLOGY	78–94	14–16	
Interpersonal Psychology			Harry Stack Sullivan
			Erik Berne, Trans- actional Analysis
Existentialism			
Humanism			

Tchr's guide ___ x ___

Producer Human Relations Media	Distributor	Grade level 10+
Release date __1980__ Format	6 fs. & cass.	Price $ 115

Source	Date	Page	Remarks*
Producer			
Clark		5	self-actualization, Gestalt: Rollo May, Laing, Maslow,
Ch.Ctr.			Rogers
SSSS			
Core Coll.			
ESLC			
MRD			
Horn			
SLJ			
Sci.Bks	March–April	81	"highly recommended," outstanding visuals and narration
Booklist			
NICEM			
Other (name Previews 5/79			

Abbreviations:
        Ch.Ctr.   Children's Book and Music Center
        ESLC   Elementary School Library Collection
        Horn   Guide to Simulations/Games
        MRD   Media Review Digest
        SSSS   Social Studies School Service
        Sci.Bks.   Science Books and Films

*Record here quotes, references to alternative titles,
 other considerations for selection decisions

SELECTION WORKSHEET

Set	Title	Size ## of pages ## of frames	Running Time	Contents Remarks*
155.2	BASIC CONCEPTS IN PSYCHOLOGY			
Segments	The Psychoanalytic Viewpoint			
	The Behaviorist Viewpoint			
	The Cognitive Viewpoint			
	The Humanistic Viewpoint			

Tchr's guide ___X___
Producer __Prentice-Hall Media__   Distributor _____   Grade level __7–12__
Release date __1978__   Format __4 fs. & cass.__   Price __$ 119__

Source	Date	Page	Remarks*
Producer			
Clark	81/82	10	leaders, principles, methods
Ch.Ctr.			
SSSS			
Core Coll.			
ESLC			
MRD	1979	no	
Horn			
SLJ			
Sci.Bks			
Booklist	80/81	no	
NICEM			
Other (name)			

Abbreviations:

Ch.Ctr.	Children's Book and Music Center
ESLC	Elementary School Library Collection
Horn	Guide to Simulations/Games
MRD	Media Review Digest
SSSS	Social Studies School Service
Sci.Bks.	Science Books and Films

*Record here quotes, references to alternative titles, other considerations for selection decisions

SELECTION WORKSHEET

Set	Title	Size ## of pages ## of frames	Running Time	Contents Remarks*
150.19 LANDMARKS IN PSYCHOLOGY				
Segments				

Tchr's guide _____

Producer Human Relations Media | Distributor _____ | Grade level 7-12

Release date 1976 | Format 3 fs. & cass. | Price $ 115

Source	Date	Page	Remarks*
Producer			
Clark		6	Freud, Adler, Jung, Pavlov, Watson, Skinner
Ch.Ctr.			
SSSS			
Core Coll.			
ESLC			
MRD	1978	358	rec. by Previews 3/77, Media and Methods 4/77
Horn			
SLJ			
Sci.Bks			
Booklist	11/1/76		
NICEM			
Other (name)			

Abbreviations:
Ch.Ctr.	Children's Book and Music Center
ESLC	Elementary School Library Collection
Horn	Guide to Simulations/Games
MRD	Media Review Digest
SSSS	Social Studies School Service
Sci.Bks.	Science Books and Films

*Record here quotes, references to alternative titles,
other considerations for selection decisions

EXAMPLE NO. 4 (TEACHER REQUEST)

PROBLEM   The media center is unable to fill request by primary teachers for audiovisuals on nutrition and consumer education. The teachers view the two subjects as highly interrelated for this age level and are preparing an integrated unit.

STRATEGY   Two selective listings in *Curriculum Review* for April 1980 and September 1980 (see p. 127) appear to be quite in point and can serve as starting points. Budgeted amount is $150.

PRELIMINARY
SELECTION

1. Critical sources

The following appear to be likely candidates from a perusal of "Buyer Beware," the September 1980 consumer education column:

> *Nutrition and Consumer Advertising* (Pied Piper, 1979. $68.00; $25.00 each). The media specialist recognizes the title of one of the films from which these filmstrips were adapted.

> *Consumer Education: A Guide for Young People* (Q-Ed, 1977. $99.50). It is not clear from the text whether food and nutrition are discussed in this set.

The April 1980 column "Watching Your Health" yields:

> *Nutrition for Children* (Polished Apple, 1976. $70.00);

> *The Snacking Mouse* (Polished Apple, 1977. $25.00); and

> *It's What You Eat* from the *All About You* television series (AIT, 1974. $110.00).

2. Noncritical sources

No recent releases for this age group show up in the Charles W. Clark catalog.

One of the teachers sees an advertisement for a new Walt Disney multimedia kit *Nutrition around the Clock*, but since its price alone would tie up the entire budget, it is dismissed from consideration.

With five solid possibilities, teachers and media specialist agree there is no need to extend the search.

**FINAL
SELECTION**   When the two filmstrips from Polished Apple are requested for preview, the producer advises of a sequel, *Snacking Mouse Goes to School*, released 1981 ($30.00). That title is added to the preview list. The unit will be timed to the broadcast of *It's What You Eat* on the local educational channel. The media specialist makes a note to check with the local school television service to find out if and when that particular segment is to be broadcast in the current school year.

Forms and worksheets for this example follow below and on pages 149 through 153.

NEEDS ASSESSMENT FORM

SUBJECT OR TOPIC unit combining nutrition and consumer education		BUDGETED AMOUNT $150		
OBJECTIVES	Cognitive X	Affective X		Motor
INSTRUCTIONAL LEVEL(S) grade 2		STUDENT CHARACTERISTICS all		

EXPECTED USAGE,   Media Center _____   Number of Students ____85____

Classroom ___X_____   Length of Time ___6 weeks___

Date Needed January 1982

DESIRED ATTRIBUTES	Visual X	Audio	Projection X	Color X	Motion X
HOW ORIGINATED	Teacher X Student _____		Administrator _____ Media Specialist _____		

SELECTION WORKSHEET

Set / Title	Size ## of pages ## of frames	Running Time	Contents Remarks*
NUTRITION AND CONSUMER ADVERTISING	90 each	12 – 17	
Soopergoop			satire on TV commercial
Eat, Drink and be Wary			expose
Buy, Buy			

Tchr's guide _____

Producer __Pied Piper__		Distributor	Grade level 3+
Release date __1979__	Format	3 fs	Price $27 each

Source	Date	Page	Remarks*
Producer	x		
Clark	81/82	no	
Ch.Ctr.			
SSSS			
Core Coll.			
ESLC	1979	no	
MRD			
Horn			
SLJ			-
Sci.Bks			
Booklist	80/81	no	
NICEM			
Other (name) Curriculum Review	9/80		

Abbreviations:
- Ch.Ctr.   Children's Book and Music Center
- ESLC   Elementary School Library Collection
- Horn   Guide to Simulations/Games
- MRD   Media Review Digest
- SSSS   Social Studies School Service
- Sci.Bks.   Science Books and Films

*Record here quotes, references to alternative titles, other considerations for selection decisions

SELECTION WORKSHEET

Set	Title	Size ## of pages ## of frames	Running Time	Contents Remarks*
NUTRITION FOR CHILDREN		45–60	7–12min.	
Segments	The Nutrient Express			cautionary tale
	George Gorge and Nicky P.			" "
	Break the Fast			importance of breakfast

Tchr's guide __X__

Producer __Polished Apple__		Distributor		Grade level __K–2__
Release date __1976__	Format			Price __$69.75__
Source	Date	__3 fs. & cass.__		

Source	Date	Page	Remarks*
Producer		x	cartoons: recommended by Journal of Nutrition Education
Clark	81/82	no	
Ch.Ctr.			
SSSS			
Core Coll.	Elem.	no	
ESLC	1979	no	
MRD	1978–1979	no	
Horn			
SLJ			
Sci.Bks			
Booklist			
NICEM			
Other (name) Curriculum Review 4/80 four food groups			

Abbreviations:

Ch.Ctr.	Children's Book and Music Center
ESLC	Elementary School Library Collection
Horn	Guide to Simulations/Games
MRD	Media Review Digest
SSSS	Social Studies School Service
Sci.Bks.	Science Books and Films

*Record here quotes, references to alternative titles,
other considerations for selection decisions

SELECTION WORKSHEET

Set	Title	Size ## of pages ## of frames	Running Time	Contents Remarks*
	CONSUMER EDUCATION: A GUIDE FOR YOUNG PEOPLE	67–74	10–12	
640.73	Needs and Wants			
Segments	Shopping for Toys			
	Packaging and Labeling			
	A Word from the Sponsor			Good and bad TV ads
	Values and Lifestyles			
	Consumer Ecology			

Tchr's guide _____
Producer __Q-Ed__   Distributor _____   Grade level __1-6__
Release date __1977__ Format __6 fs. & cass.__   Price $ __109__

Source	Date	Page	Remarks*
Producer	x		visual shows child examining cereal box
Clark	81/82	151	
Ch.Ctr.			
SSSS			
Core Coll.			
ESLC	1979	no	
MRD	1979	301	rec. by Previews 5/78, p. 11
Horn			
SLJ			
Sci.Bks			
Booklist			
NICEM			
Other (name) Curriculum Review	9/80		

Abbreviations:
Ch.Ctr.	Children's Book and Music Center
ESLC	Elementary School Library Collection
Horn	Guide to Simulations/Games
MRD	Media Review Digest
SSSS	Social Studies School Service
Sci.Bks.	Science Books and Films

*Record here quotes, references to alternative titles, other considerations for selection decisions

SELECTION WORKSHEET

Set	Title	Size ## of pages ## of frames	Running Time	Contents Remarks*
	It's What You Eat (All About You)		15 min.	
Segments				

Tchr's guide _____

Producer ___ AIT	Distributor		Grade level 1-2
Release date 1974	Format video		Price $110

Source	Date	Page	Remarks*
Producer	1982	8	four basic food groups, balanced diet
Clark			
Ch.Ctr.			
SSSS			
Core Coll.			
ESLC			
MRD			
Horn			
SLJ			
Sci.Bks			
Booklist			
NICEM			
Other (name) Curriculum Review 4/80			find out date of local educational broadcast

Abbreviations:

Ch.Ctr.	Children's Book and Music Center
ESLC	Elementary School Library Collection
Horn	Guide to Simulations/Games
MRD	Media Review Digest
SSSS	Social Studies School Service
Sci.Bks.	Science Books and Films

*Record here quotes, references to alternative titles,
other considerations for selection decisions

SELECTION WORKSHEET

Title		Size ## of pages ## of frames	Running Time	Contents Remarks*
	Set			
641.1 THE SNACKING MOUSE		41	5	
Segments				

Tchr's guide _____

Producer __Polished Apple__   Distributor _____   Grade level __K–2__

Release date __1977__   Format 1 fs & cass.   Price __$24.75__

Source	Date	Page	Remarks*
Producer	x		cartoon format
Clark	81/82	no	
Ch.Ctr.			
SSSS			
Core Coll.			
ESLC			
MRD	1978		several recommendations
Horn			
SLJ			
Sci.Bks			
Booklist	7/15/77	1740	
NICEM			
Other (name) Curriculum Review 4/80			cautionary tale about sweets and fats

Abbreviations:
Ch.Ctr.	Children's Book and Music Center
ESLC	Elementary School Library Collection
Horn	Guide to Simulations/Games
MRD	Media Review Digest
SSSS	Social Studies School Service
Sci.Bks.	Science Books and Films

*Record here quotes, references to alternative titles, other considerations for selection decisions

EXAMPLE NO. 5 (TEACHER/MEDIA SPECIALIST-INITIATED)

PROBLEM   The concern is to supplement the ninth-grade world cultures text with visuals of ancient Chinese art works which were only recently excavated.

STRATEGY   "China: Past, Present, and Future" appeared in the December 1979 issue of *Previews*. The media specialist will look it over before consulting with the art department. Budget is $25.00.

PRELIMINARY
SELECTION   *China: Its Future in Its Past?* (Pathescope, 1980) sounds, from its description, as though it might fit the need exactly. Critical sources note only films on the subject.

The art department offers to contact the Education Division of the Metropolitan Museum of Art, and thus learns of a $20.00 set of 40 slides with narration based on the museum's exhibit, "The Great Bronze Age of China."

FINAL
SELECTION   The producer advises that *China: Its Future in Its Past?* has been both delayed and also renamed *China and Its Pottery Army*. At $75.00, it exceeds the budgeted amount and its subject coverage appears similar to the museum slide set. The latter is ordered sight unseen.

A form for this example follows below.

NEEDS ASSESSMENT FORM

SUBJECT OR TOPIC China - recent archaeological discoveries		BUDGETED AMOUNT $25		
OBJECTIVES	Cognitive	Affective to gain appreciation for 4000-year continuity of Ch.culture		Motor
INSTRUCTIONAL LEVEL(S) 9th grade World Cultures course		STUDENT CHARACTERISTICS all		
EXPECTED USAGE	Media Center _____ Classroom ___x___ Date Needed ___Nov. 1___	Number of Students 300 Length of Time 8 weeks		
DESIRED ATTRIBUTES	Visual x	Audio	Projection	Color	Motion
HOW ORIGINATED	Teacher _____ Student _____	Administrator _____ Media Specialist _____		

EXAMPLE NO. 6 (COMPUTER-RELATED)

PROBLEM   The school district has purchased microcomputers for each building and has adopted a policy of integrating computer use and computer literacy into as many curriculum area as possible. Professional staff as well as students from grade 4 up are targets of the computer literacy program. The district media resources center is allotted $1000 for the 1981/1982 school year for the purchase of instructional materials that address 1) what computers are and can do; 2) programming and BASIC language; 3) societal effects of computers; 4) software evaluation.

STRATEGY   The media specialist knows from glancing at catalogs coming across the desk that many distributors are featuring new programs that cater to this need being felt in many districts. Though the budgeted amount is generous, it must stretch for all instructional levels and also for staff use. Comparison shopping is definitely indicated.

PRELIMINARY SELECTION

1. Critical sources

Core Media Collection for Secondary Schools under "Computers" lists several 1973-1976 releases, the most recent one being

> *Computers and Human Society* (Sunburst, 1976. 6FS & cassettes, 77-102 fr., 14-19 min. each).

Core Media Collection for Elementary Schools yields

> *Computers: From Pebbles to Programs* (Guidance Associates, 1975. 3 FS & cassettes, 63-97 fr., 11-13 min. each); there are no cross-references to anything else. The same title also is in the *Elementary School Library Collection* (12th ed. 1979), which has nothing more recent to recommend.

A search of the title indexes in February and August 1981 issues of *Booklist* leads to reviews of books only. The index in the December 1981 issue of *School Library Journal* proves another dead end. *Science Books and Films* reviewed no computer filmstrips between September 1980 and October 1981.

2. Noncritical sources

School Library Journal's September 1981 "AV Forecast" includes a substantial section on computers, summarizing releases from a half dozen vendors, including:

> *Basic Computer Literacy* (Eye Gate Media. 4 FS & 2 cassettes, 50-52 fr., 10-12 min. each. $68.00; $15.00each FS, $10.00 each cassette. Gr. 7-12);

Computer Awareness (Society for Visual Education. 4 FS & cassettes, 60 fr., 12 min. each. $125.00; $18.00 each FS, $12.00 each cassette; $185.00 with two discs for TRS-80 or 32K Apple II. Gr. 5-12);

Computer Literacy: The First Step (Educational Dimensions Group. 4 FS & cassettes, appr. 70-80 fr., 18-20 min. each. $146.00; $36.50 each. Gr. 7-12);

Computer Programming (Bergwall. 4 FS & cassettes, 60-65 fr., 12-15 min. each. $129.00; $42.50 each. Gr. 9-12);

Introduction to Computers: Basic Computer Background (Eye Gate. 4 FS & 2 cassettes, 50-52 fr., 10-12 min. each. $68.00; $15.00 each FS, $10.00 each cassette. Gr. 7-12);

Introduction to Data Processing (Educational Audiovisual. 3 FS & cassettes, 60-80 fr., 12-15 min. each. $106.00. Gr. 7-12);

Introduction to Systems Analysis and Programming (Educational Audiovisual. 3 FS & cassettes, 60-80 fr., 12-15 min. each. $106.00. Gr. 7-12).

The Charles W. Clark catalog's subject index produces *Computers and Human Society* (see above) and a transparency set, *Data Processing*, of unknown date. Several Dewey Decimal numbers can pertain to this subject. None proved productive. The following titles were noted for purposes of comparison with more current ones:

Careers in Electronics (Library Filmstrip Center, 1979. 1 FS & cassette, 60 fr., 18 min. $30.00. Gr. 10-12);

Computer Concepts (RMI Media Productions, n.d. 3 FS & cassettes. $96.00; $35.00 each. Gr. 7-12);

Digital Computer Fundamentals (Projected Learning Programs, n.d. 5 FS & cassettes. $162.50; $32.50 each. Gr. 10 up).

Previews' October 1980 "AV Guide" (the forerunner of the *SLJ* "AV Forecast" feature) tipped the searchers off to:

Society and the Chip (Educational Audiovisual. 2 FS & cassettes, $60.00. Gr. 10 up) (listed under "Social Studies—General");

BASIC for Microcomputers (Educational Activities. 5 FS & cassettes. $89.00. Gr. 5 up);

BASIC: An Introduction to Computer Programming (Center for Humanities. 2 FS & cassettes, $139.50 or 160 slides, $159.50. Gr. 7-12).

Checking the distributor catalogs for these programs revealed yet another one:

Advanced BASIC Techniques (Educational Activities. 5 FS & 4 cassettes. $74.00).

Checking the three reviewing journals one more time confirmed that none of these programs had received critical evaluations in any of the publications.

FINAL SELECTION

With no reviews ,to help narrow the choices, there was no alternative but to request all the programs for simultaneous previewing by a broad-based committee. Before embarking on its previewing assignment, the committee spent one session defining with specificity the desired contents coverage and priorities. The nod went to materials of a cognitive nature and suitable for individual study. A special evaluation form was devised adding these factors to the criteria generally endorsed by the district.

A further determination resulted in allotting $100 of the budgeted amount toward the rental of films, especially films demonstrating computer graphics, which by its nature cannot be demonstrated by still-visual media, as well as films offering comment on the power and human impact of technology.

Forms and worksheets for this example follow below and on pages 158 through 166.

NEEDS ASSESSMENT FORM

SUBJECT OR TOPIC	computer literacy computer programming computers in society		BUDGETED AMOUNT		$1000		
OBJECTIVES	Cognitive x			Affective			Motor
INSTRUCTIONAL LEVEL(S)	grades 4–12 professional staff		STUDENT CHARACTERISTICS		broad range		
EXPECTED USAGE	Media Center __x__ Classroom _____ Date Needed __1/82__		Number of Students _1500_ Length of Time __all year__				
DESIRED ATTRIBUTES	Visual x	Audio x	Projection x		Color x		Motion x
HOW ORIGINATED	Teacher _____ Student _____		Administrator __x__ Media Specialist _ _ _____				

SELECTION WORKSHEET

	Title	Size ## of pages ## of frames	Running Time	Contents Remarks*
Set				
Segments	Advanced BASIC Techniques			
	String Functions			
	Data Handling and Arrays			sorting
	Computer Graphics and Misc. Functions			
	Adv. Mathemtical Functions			

Tchr's guide X

Producer Educational Activities			Distributor	Grade level
Release date 1980		Format	5fs, 4 cass.	Price $74

Source	Date	Page	Remarks*
Producer			
Clark			
Ch.Ctr.			
SSSS			
Core Coll.			
ESLC			
MRD			
Horn			
SLJ			
Sci.Bks			
Booklist			
NICEM			
Other (name)			

Abbreviations:

Ch.Ctr.	Children's Book and Music Center
ESLC	Elementary School Library Collection
Horn	Guide to Simulations/Games
MRD	Media Review Digest
SSSS	Social Studies School Service
Sci.Bks.	Science Books and Films

*Record here quotes, references to alternative titles, other considerations for selection decisions

SELECTION WORKSHEET

Set	Title	Size ## of pages ## of frames	Running Time	Contents Remarks*
	BASIC: An Introduction to			key words & concepts
	Computer Programming	160 total		intro to vocabulary
Segments				simple programming techniques
				flow charts
				creation of programs

Tchr's guide __X__

Producer		Distributor Ctr.for Humanit.	Grade level 7-12
Release date 1980?	Format 2 fs & cass or discs,160 slides		Price $139.50;159.50 (SL)

Source	Date	Page	Remarks*
Producer			
Clark	81/82	no	
Ch.Ctr.			
SSSS			
Core Coll.			
ESLC			
MRD			
Horn			
SLJ			
Sci.Bks			
Booklist			
NICEM			
Other (name)			

Abbreviations:

Ch.Ctr.	Children's Book and Music Center
ESLC	Elementary School Library Collection
Horn	Guide to Simulations/Games
MRD	Media Review Digest
SSSS	Social Studies School Service
Sci.Bks.	Science Books and Films

*Record here quotes, references to alternative titles,
other considerations for selection decisions

SELECTION WORKSHEET

Set	Title	Size ## of pages ## of frames	Running Time	Contents Remarks*
BASIC for Microcomputers				
	Getting Started w/the Computer			
Segments	Mathematical Operations			
	Loops and Subroutines			
	Intro. to Original Programming			
	Progr.Techniques and Flow charts			

Tchr's guide incl.script, programs, student activities, answers

Producer			Distributor Educ.Activ.	Grade level 5+
Release date 1979		Format 5 fs & cass.		Price $89

Source	Date	Page	Remarks*
Producer			for PET,Apple,TRS-80;sequential;incl. worksheets
Clark			
Ch.Ctr.			
SSSS			
Core Coll.			
ESLC			
MRD			
Horn			
SLJ			
Sci.Bks			
Booklist			
NICEM			
Other (name)			

Abbreviations:

Ch.Ctr.	Children's Book and Music Center
ESLC	Elementary School Library Collection
Horn	Guide to Simulations/Games
MRD	Media Review Digest
SSSS	Social Studies School Service
Sci.Bks.	Science Books and Films

*Record here quotes, references to alternative titles, other considerations for selection decisions

SELECTION WORKSHEET

Set	Title	Size ## of pages ## of frames	Running Time	Contents Remarks*
	COMPUTERS AND HUMAN SOCIETY	77-102each	14-19 each	
Segments	The Ultimate Servant			Middle Ages to present
	The Electronic Brain			How it works; cartoons
	The Evolution of Intelligence			Artificial intelligence
	The Computer Revolution			Effect on society
	The Data Explosion&Central Control			Control of data may = power
	Projections for Man and Machine			Speculation; space exploration

Tchr's guide _____

Producer _____   Distributor Sunburst   Grade level 8-12

Release date __1976__   Format 6 fs & cass.   Price $169

Source	Date	Page	Remarks*
Producer			
Clark	x	160	
Ch.Ctr.			
SSSS			
Core Coll.	x		
ESLC			
MRD	1978	351	
Horn			
SLJ			
Sci.Bks			
Booklist	6/15/77	1584	art reproductions, good visuals&music, "provocative"
NICEM			
Other (name)	Previews,12/77,17		"sound...intriguing," computer/human similarities emphasized, so-so visuals

Abbreviations:
Ch.Ctr.	Children's Book and Music Center
ESLC	Elementary School Library Collection
Horn	Guide to Simulations/Games
MRD	Media Review Digest
SSSS	Social Studies School Service
Sci.Bks.	Science Books and Films

*Record here quotes, references to alternative titles,
other considerations for selection decisions

SELECTION WORKSHEET

Set	Title	Size ## of pages ## of frames	Running Time	Contents Remarks*
	COMPUTERS FROM PEBBLES TO PROGRAMS	63–97	11–13	
Segments	Part I			abacus through 1930s
	Part II			WWII to present
	Part III			efficiency of computers
				computer applications

Tchr's guide _____

Producer **Guidance Associates**   Distributor **Ctr.for Humanit.**   Grade level **5–8**

Release date **1975**   Format _____   Price **$199.50**

Source	Date	Page	Remarks*
Producer			
Clark	81/82	no	
Ch.Ctr.			
SSSS			
Core Coll.	x		
ESLC	x		
MRD	1977		rec. by Math Teacher 11/76, Learning 12/76
Horn		/	
SLJ			
Sci.Bks			
Booklist			
NICEM			
Other (name)			

Abbreviations:

Ch.Ctr.	Children's Book and Music Center
ESLC	Elementary School Library Collection
Horn	Guide to Simulations/Games
MRD	Media Review Digest
SSSS	Social Studies School Service
Sci.Bks.	Science Books and Films

*Record here quotes, references to alternative titles,
other considerations for selection decisions

SELECTION WORKSHEET

Set	Title	Size ## of pages ## of frames	Running Time	Contents Remarks*
	SOCIETY AND THE CHIP	100-114	15-18 min.	Issues for Troubled Times series
Segments				Development of micro- electronics and impact for future

Tchr's guide __X__

Producer _____ Distributor Educ.Audiovisual Grade level 10-12

Release date __1980__ Format 2 fs & cass. Price __$60__

Source	Date	Page	Remarks*
Producer			
Clark	81/82	no	
Ch.Ctr.			
SSSS			
Core Coll.			
ESLC			
MRD			
Horn			
SLJ			
Sci.Bks			
Booklist	80/81	no	
NICEM			
Other (name)			

Abbreviations:

Ch.Ctr.	Children's Book and Music Center
ESLC	Elementary School Library Collection
Horn	Guide to Simulations/Games
MRD	Media Review Digest
SSSS	Social Studies School Service
Sci.Bks.	Science Books and Films

*Record here quotes, references to alternative titles,
other considerations for selection decisions

SELECTION WORKSHEET

Set	Title	Size ## of pages ## of frames	Running Time	Contents Remarks*
<u>DATA PROCESSING</u>				
Segments				

Tchr's guide ___ X

Producer ___ Milliken	Distributor	Grade level ___ 7+
Release date ____	Format 12 transp., 16 ditto masters	Price $ 12.95

Source	Date	Page	Remarks*
Producer			
Clark	81/82	160	
Ch.Ctr.			
SSSS			
Core Coll.			
ESLC			
MRD			
Horn			
SLJ			
Sci.Bks			
Booklist			
NICEM			
Other (name)			

Abbreviations:

Ch.Ctr.	Children's Book and Music Center
ESLC	Elementary School Library Collection
Horn	Guide to Simulations/Games
MRD	Media Review Digest
SSSS	Social Studies School Service
Sci.Bks.	Science Books and Films

*Record here quotes, references to alternative titles,
other considerations for selection decisions

SELECTION WORKSHEET

Set / Title	Size ## of pages ## of frames	Running Time	Contents Remarks*
JOBS FOR THE 80s: WHERE THE OPPORTUNITIES ARE	240		7 most promising occupational areas
Segments			

Tchr's guide __X__
Producer Guidance Associates   Distributor Ctr.for Human.   Grade level 7-12
Release date 1980?   Format 2 fs & cass.or discs or slides   Price $179.50; $199.50 (SL)

Source	Date	Page	Remarks*
Producer			
Clark		no	
Ch.Ctr.			
SSSS			
Core Coll.			
ESLC			
MRD			
Horn			
SLJ			
Sci.Bks			
Booklist			
NICEM	1980	no	
Other (name) Previews AV Guide	10/80, p. 67		

Abbreviations:

Ch.Ctr.	Children's Book and Music Center
ESLC	Elementary School Library Collection
Horn	Guide to Simulations/Games
MRD	Media Review Digest
SSSS	Social Studies School Service
Sci.Bks.	Science Books and Films

*Record here quotes, references to alternative titles, other considerations for selection decisions

Conclusion

The six randomly selected examples in chapter 14 demonstrate, it is hoped, that judicious use of selection aids pays off. In not one of the cases could equally useful selections have been made simply by examining a handful of catalogs or a few convention exhibits. Nor was the process very difficult in any of the cases. The procedures suggested in this text will become almost automatic after they have been followed a few times. Shortcuts or other improvements may present themselves in the process.

If the selection process outlined here is followed, the resultant collection will satisfy the demand of the instructional development process. Teachers will be able to find instructional materials for specific uses and that will meet specific purposes. Funds will be spent to the best advantage and waste will be avoided. The approval rating of the library/media center should see a healthy increase and its staff take satisfaction in improved performance.

Index